BLACK HOMEOWNERSHIP
on MARTHA'S VINEYARD

BLACK HOMEOWNERSHIP
on MARTHA'S VINEYARD
A HISTORY

THOMAS DRESSER AND RICHARD LEWIS TAYLOR

THE
History
PRESS

Published by The History Press
Charleston, SC
www.historypress.com

Front cover top, left to right: Black-owned Campground cottages of Reverend Jackson, Helen Peck, and Dorothy West. *Bottom*: Shearer Cottage guests and employees gathered in 1931. Adam Clayton Powell Jr. stands on the left; Charles Shearer is third from right. Lillian Evanti, world-renowned Black opera singer, leans in on the back row. *Courtesy of Lee Van Allen, historian of the Shearer family.*

Back cover, inset: The Goldsberry siblings. *Bottom*: Jocelyn Coleman with her grandmother, 1940.

First published 2024
Updated 2024

Manufactured in the United States

ISBN 9781467157070

Library of Congress Control Number: 2024931860

IN MEMORIA

People in this project lost family members and friends. We respect and remember.

Marie Allen
David Coleman
Jay Coleman
Deborah Dixon
Randall Taylor
Duncan Walton

Our thoughts and prayers are with their families. We share their grief and recall their contributions to our lives and the community.

CONTENTS

CONTENTS

FOREWORD

AN INTERVIEW WITH JOCELYN COLEMAN WALTON ON LEGACY HOMEOWNERSHIP

Jocelyn Coleman Walton and her four siblings enjoyed summers with friends and family in The Highlands thanks to their grandmother Luella Barnett Coleman. Jocelyn's grandmother came to the Island in the 1920s as a domestic and spent many summers working for others. Every summer, as soon as school closed, Granny brought the kids to the Island for the whole summer.

Luella and her husband, Ralf, were working-class people. We asked Jocelyn Coleman about her grandparents. "My grandfather was a presser in Boston's garment district, even though he was very involved in Boston's Negro Theatre, from acting to directing. But you couldn't make money in the theatre, especially if you were Black."

Jocelyn and her four siblings each had two children. Her aunt's two daughters had four children between them. So, Luella and Ralf had fourteen great-grandchildren. They called themselves "The Cousins," and whenever they were together, there was lots of laughter and lots of talk on the importance of Coleman Corners and keeping it in the family. "That's what Black legacy homeownership is all about," said Jocelyn.

Jocelyn said, "Kyle, one of my sons, was walking up Myrtle Avenue, and said, 'It is home to me.'" She continued. "He, and the other great-grandchildren, are very committed to holding onto the property; it is an honored legacy. The Cousins have talked about one day purchasing the two properties on Coleman Corners that have been sold off."

As teenagers, Jocelyn and her friends called themselves the Hound Dogs. "We were just regular kids, swimming at the Inkwell and enjoying the activity of Circuit Avenue." More recently, Jocelyn and her sisters had an annual "Hen Party," where the ladies of the Hound Dogs would gather, years after their childhood hijinks. "The Hound Dogs share a cherished history of 'coming of age,' and continue to support each other," added Jocelyn.

We asked what life would have been like had her grandmother not brought her to The Highlands.

"I would have missed out on the sense of freedom, the sense of belonging. I think back on some of the people I've known who didn't have similar opportunities, and I see how limited my life experience could have been.

"Roxbury, where I grew up, was integrated so I never felt uncomfortable among whites. But I also never felt a sense of being part of a community. Spending summers in The Highlands provided that. Here was a neighborhood of people who looked like us. We weren't aware of their social status. We only knew that they were receptive and supportive. That sense of belonging and being valued expands your horizons, it helps to mold you into the person you're going to be.

"We had so much love and respect for my grandmother, and her trust in us allowed us so much freedom. Once we did our chores, we were free to spread our wings. Mornings at the Tabernacle attending Bible School, days at the Inkwell Beach and, later, as teenagers spending evenings on Circuit Avenue." She paused. "As a young teenager, I received a church scholarship to spend a week at a summer camp. I completed the week, but it was not the same. Paradise was here.

"A group of students from California were on Island recently, studying climate change. They asked me about going to a Black college. I said that I grew up proud of being a Coleman. At Morgan State, I became proud to be an African American. As I think about the impact of spending summers on Myrtle Avenue, I realize that sense of pride began in The Highlands, among the Black families who demonstrated respect, concern, and interest in the five Coleman siblings.

"Give your children the opportunity to spend enough quality time here to build meaningful connections…to the place and its people." She concluded, "That's my suggestion to promote Black legacy homeownership."

PREFACE

Our goal in *Black Homeownership on Martha's Vineyard: A History* is to review the legacy of houses owned by Blacks and passed on through future generations on Martha's Vineyard.

Black Homeownership on Martha's Vineyard is a response to several issues. Has Black homeownership on the Vineyard eroded over the years, as it has in comparable Black communities like Idlewild, Michigan, and Sag Harbor, New York? We recognize the growth of Black families who live year-round on the Vineyard. And we discuss the disclosure by the Camp Meeting Association in Oak Bluffs that their leadership in the late nineteenth century displaced a small community of Black people from their homes. We share their backstory.

National events colored racial activities in the early twentieth century. And we explore the role property has played in the history of voting.

This book is an exposé, both revealing and cathartic.

We commend Black families who held legacy property through the years, through the generations, through the bad times and good.

Family trees of several families are listed in the appendix, provided by Jane Meleney Coe, who authored *A Guide to East Chop Families*. Of this project, she wrote, "I really appreciate what you are doing in more ways than one. What I got from it is that you are taking information which leaves everyone feeling outraged and sad and following up with more context and what came next. Recognize, accept, even honor the hurt and harm, but move on from there."

PREFACE

We supplement the story with contributions by people who brought their experience to the fore. Jocelyn Coleman, of The Highlands, shared memories of summering in Oak Bluffs. Jeffrey Burnett added his expertise as a historical architectural student, researching the Baptist Tabernacle. Shelley Christiansen, a Vineyard realtor, offered her perspective on legacy homeownership. Also, we include perspectives by Barbara Edelin and Bijan Bayne that offer perspective on our study.

ACKNOWLEDGEMENTS

The families who shared their stories deserve our sincere appreciation for opening their hearts, their homes, and their histories. We want to thank Carroll and Myrna Allston; Beth Bago; Julia Burgess; Jocelyn Coleman Walton; Debbie Dixon; Barbara Edelin; James and Carol Goldsberry; James, Janice, and Jody Hubert; Abby McGrath; Margaret Olivera; Shera Toledo; Olive Tomlinson; Gretchen Tucker-Underwood; Lee Van Allen; and Jo-Ann Walker.

Shera Toledo commented: "My mother always loved and supported your work. Thank you for writing about my family."

The Appendix of Family Trees was provided by Jane Meleney Coe in her *East Chop Family Guides*.

Bow Van Riper, librarian of the Martha's Vineyard Museum, shared his expertise.

The able and affable library staff in Oak Bluffs always stands by, ready to assist.

Hilary Wallcox, librarian of the *Vineyard Gazette*, shared her expertise with timely responses.

Jeffrey Burnett added his report on the Baptist Tabernacle.

Shelley Christiansen shared her expertise as a realtor, a historian and one with a keen eye on Vineyarders.

Jocelyn Coleman Walton shared poignant parts of her family's history.

Paulo DeOliveira at the Registry of Deeds opened the books of past practices in real estate.

ACKNOWLEDGEMENTS

Attorney Rachel Orr offered insight on restrictive covenants.

Andrew Patch uncovered the practices of nineteenth-century Camp Meeting Association affairs.

Once more, The History Press supported an endeavor to explore Vineyard history. Mike Kinsella excels as the acquisitions editor. Abigail Fleming is a superb senior copy editor. Dani McGrath and Samantha Linnane work diligently to distribute this book. Our thanks for all their efforts.

Joyce Dresser provided myriad photographs AND pinpoint editing AND endless hours of support and encouragement in this project.

1

LANDOWNERSHIP

I n the beginning, before the American Revolution, colonists associated democracy with disorder and mob rule. They believed the right to vote should be restricted to those who owned property or paid taxes. In their view, only sufficiently independent, committed members of the community should vote. Each of the thirteen colonies required voters to either own a certain amount of land or personal property or pay a specified amount in taxes.

White men with property were the only people allowed to vote in colonial America. Certain classes of residents faced restrictions. Women, Blacks and Native Americans could not vote. Five colonies restricted Catholics from voting; four colonies denied the franchise to Jews.

Colonists believed owning property was a prerequisite to the right to vote. Unfortunately, limiting the vote to those who owned property meant poor people did not participate in the electoral process. Voting was limited to men with money. It was inferred that the poor, enslaved or female were unqualified to vote.

Vermont was the first state to eliminate all restrictions on voters.

James Madison, father of the Constitution, struggled with the challenges of expanding the right to vote. "The right of suffrage is a fundamental Article in Republican Constitutions," he wrote. "The regulation of it is, at the same time, a task of peculiar delicacy. Allow the right [to vote] exclusively to property [owners], and the rights of persons may be oppressed....Extend it equally to all, and the rights of property [owners]...may be overruled by a majority without property."[1]

Voting in colonial America was based on the premise that voters should have a "stake in society."

The right to vote is the most important right of citizenship. It involves a reasoned participation in our future. It should include all adults capable of determining the best choice in an election.

The history of suffrage in the United States has been tied to property, to land, to homeownership. Holding property is legacy homeownership.

The Library of Congress affirms that "the 1965 Voting Rights Act created a significant change in the status of African Americans throughout the South. The Voting Rights Act prohibited the states from using literacy tests and other methods of excluding African Americans from voting. Prior to this, only an estimated twenty-three percent of voting-age blacks were registered nationally, but by 1969 the number had jumped to sixty-one percent."

Holding a family house at least two generations is "legacy property" in the Black community. If that property is sold to another Black family, it is a "legacy leap property." If it is sold to a white family, it is a "legacy lost."

A home is not only shelter but an asset as well. It can be used to send a family's children to college or an equity line of credit for an entrepreneurial project. Generational wealth is based on retention of property.

Beyond the value of property itself, barriers of racial discrimination that impeded Black homeownership on the mainland were overcome to a great degree on Martha's Vineyard.

THE "OAK BLUFFS TOWN crier…walked the streets of town in the late 1800s, ringing a bell and calling out the news of the day."[2] REVEREND WILLIAM JACKSON was town crier in the 1890s.

Reverend Jackson initially rented a Campground cottage at 12 Central Avenue in 1870; the next year, he bought it. His house sits across Lake Avenue from Nancy's Restaurant. He owned the house but leased the land from the Methodists, as was and is the custom of property ownership in the Camp Meeting Association.

When Reverend Jackson passed in 1900, his daughter Mary inherited the property and held it until 1921. That amounts to half a century of Black homeownership on Martha's Vineyard. It qualifies as Black legacy homeownership. Thus, Reverend Jackson, an eminent Black man, was among the first Black homeowners on Martha's Vineyard. His house will be recognized by the African American Heritage Trail.

Reverend William Jackson bought his Campground cottage in 1871. Jackson represents one of the earliest examples of Black legacy homeownership. *Courtesy of Joyce Dresser.*

Owning a home on Martha's Vineyard, as a Black man, was not Reverend Jackson's only accomplishment. Jackson's legacy was lifelong and well deserved every step of the way.

William Jackson was born in August 1818 in Virginia. His parents, Henry Jackson Jr. and Keziah, had been manumitted. William's father was a pilot; he navigated the vessel on which the Marquis de Lafayette sailed during his triumphant return to America in 1824.

The Jacksons moved to Philadelphia in 1831 following the Nat Turner slave rebellion.

In his twenties, William Jackson volunteered in the unsegregated U.S. Navy. He served on USS *Grampus*, chasing pirates and slave ships offshore. In 1842, Jackson was ordained as a Baptist minister in Philadelphia. He was proud his African American church was the first to have a bell; whites feared a church bell would be rung if slave catchers were in the area.

When marshals arrested one of Jackson's parishioners, Jackson and a group of associates kidnapped the parishioner, dressed him in women's clothing and sent him on to Canada and freedom. Jackson was arrested, but fellow clergy managed to free him. It was time to move again.

In 1855, William Jackson relocated to New Bedford and was named minister of the Second Baptist Church. From there, Jackson visited Martha's Vineyard and Nantucket.

Frederick Douglass was active in recruiting Black soldiers for the Fifty-Fourth and Fifty-Fifth companies of Black soldiers during the Civil War. Douglass encouraged Reverend Jackson to join the Union army as chaplain for the Fifty-Fifth.

At the age of fifty-three, Jackson bought his cottage in the Martha's Vineyard Camp Meeting Association. "In July 1876, his most renowned friend Frederick Douglass was his house guest in Oak Bluffs."[3] Douglass gave a forty-five-minute speech at the Tabernacle, heralded by "Joy to the World." The *Providence Evening Press* noted, "It was a restful visit for great men."

Reverend Jackson died on May 19, 1900. He was interred at Oak Grove Cemetery, New Bedford. "And he was quite definitely one of the first great civil rights leaders to be associated with the Island of Martha's Vineyard."[4]

2

OWNING PROPERTY

Enslaved people lived on Martha's Vineyard. That is uncontested. Slavery on the Vineyard links the Island to the rest of the country.

Samuel Sarson, a grandson of Thomas Mayhew, progenitor of the Vineyard's Edgartown settlement, sold a woman for twenty pounds. Documentation of enslaved people in the early eighteenth century is housed in the Martha's Vineyard Museum.

Blacks captured on the west coast of Africa were transported to Jamestown, Virginia, beginning in 1619. The slave trade continued for two hundred years. Slavery was prevalent in the South and not unknown in the North. Slaves were considered property, not allowed to own property themselves.

Caesar's Field was across from the Martha's Vineyard Airport. The land was purchased by Caesar, an enslaved man, who bought his freedom for £15. In 1727, Peter, a ten-year-old boy, was sold by Zacheus Mayhew of Chilmark to Ebenezer Hatch of Falmouth for £150. Ebenezer Allen owned several enslaved men, valued at £200.

Slavery was not an anomaly on Martha's Vineyard.

Reverend Samuel Sewall (1652–1730) was an occasional visitor to Martha's Vineyard. He advocated for the abolition of slavery. His tract *The Selling of Joseph*, published in 1700, condemned the slave trade. Next to life itself, Sewall considered liberty the most important condition. "Man-stealing" was "an atrocious crime," wrote Sewall.

Although opposed to slavery, Sewall did support segregation, acknowledging the difference in skin color. Still, he recognized Blacks as children of God, deserving respect.

Shortly before *The Selling of Joseph* was published, he served as a judge in the Salem witch trials of the 1690s. After putting twenty accused witches to death, he recanted and acknowledged the error of his ways.

In many respects, Reverend Sewall was ahead of his time. He came to respect all human life, without regard to gender, race, or ethnicity.

———

ESTHER WAS AN ENSLAVED Native American. She was captured and secured in the hold of the *Endeavor* when it docked in Edgartown Harbor in 1743. Esther was bound in the hold, which was bolted. The ship was secured at the dock, and the crew went to sleep. In the morning, Esther had escaped. It is doubtful she could have made it without assistance, but no one was charged.

In 2020, the National Park Service recognized Edgartown as a site on the Underground Railroad. A plaque honors Esther on the observation deck in Edgartown.

The saga of Rebecca explores Vineyard Blacks in the eighteenth century. Known as Beck, she was taken from Guinea in West Africa and enslaved by Colonel Cornelius Bassett, whose Chilmark farm was by North Road and Menemsha Crossroads. Beck married Jenoxett, a Wampanoag known as Elisha Amos. Jenoxett owned land along North Road. When Jenoxett died in 1763, Rebecca inherited his land. Thus, Beck, an enslaved woman, owned property on Martha's Vineyard.

A plaque placed by the African American Trail recognizes Beck's unusual legacy. It sits atop the steps to the water at Great Rock Bight Preserve in Chilmark. A statue of Beck, by Barney Zeitz, will be placed on North Road at the Native Earth Teaching Farm in Chilmark.

Beck's children were born enslaved. When Colonel Bassett died in 1779, Beck and her children, Pero, Nancy and probably Cato, were sold at a slave auction to Joseph Allen of Tisbury. Following the Revolution, Beck and her children were freed.

———

AFRICAN AMERICAN HERITAGE TRAIL
OF MARTHA'S VINEYARD

HONORS THE STORY OF

ESTHER

ON JULY 27, 1743, IN EDGARTOWN HARBOR,
A WOMAN NAMED ESTHER ESCAPED FROM THE
SLOOP ENDEAVOR THAT WAS RETURNING HER
TO ENSLAVEMENT IN NORTH CAROLINA.

"WE BOUND HER FEET TO A CROWBAR AND TIED
HER HANDS BEHIND HER BACK AND PUT HER
DOWN IN THE HOLD AND LAID THE HATCHES.
HOW SHE GOT LOOSE, WE KNOW NOT BUT IN THE
MORNING SHE WAS GONE WITH THE SLOOP'S
LONG BOAT." DEPOSITION OF THOMAS TAYLOR,
MATE OF THE SLOOP ENDEAVOR, JULY 28, 1743

DESIGNATED AS A SITE BY THE NPS, NATIONAL
UNDERGROUND RAILROAD NETWORK TO FREEDOM

"TRUTH IS POWERFUL AND IT PREVAILS"
SOJOURNER TRUTH

The plaque on the Edgartown observation deck recognizes Esther, an enslaved woman who escaped from the ship *Endeavor* in 1743. *Courtesy of the National Park Service.*

THE FIRST CENSUS OF Martha's Vineyard was conducted in 1765. Of 2,414 people, 46 were Black, or 2 percent. A century later, in 1860, of 3,812 people, 298 were Black or 8 percent of the populace.

During the Revolution, enslaved people petitioned the Massachusetts General Court that "they might be liberated from a State of Bondage and made Free-men of the Community." George Moore, author of *Notes on the History of Slavery* reported, in 1866, "Not one of their prayers was answered."[5]

Politicians refused to address enslavement. They argued that were slavery abolished, slaveholders would lose their investment. Whites feared an influx of freed slaves would impose an undue burden on the community.

THE LIFE OF ELIZABETH Freeman (1744–1829) was worthy. "Less than one year after the adoption of the Massachusetts State Constitution, a brave enslaved woman challenged the document's proposed principles. Motivated by the promise of liberty, Elizabeth Freeman, born as 'Mum Bett,' became the first African American woman to successfully file a lawsuit for freedom in the state of Massachusetts."[6]

When Mum Bett won her case in 1781, it led to a succession of "freedom suits." That led the Massachusetts Supreme Judicial Court to determine slavery was illegal in Massachusetts.

As a free woman, Mum Bett changed her name to Elizabeth Freeman. Besides work as a domestic, she served as a midwife, a nurse, and a healer. "After 20 years, she was able to buy her own house where she lived with her children."[7]

The abolition of slavery in Massachusetts was reaffirmed in 1783. Quock Walker, a Black man taken from west Africa, was enslaved in Worcester County. Born in 1753, Walker was twenty-eight when he ran from his enslaver, Jennison, but was soon apprehended and severely beaten. Walker sued for battery, which led to the court case.

Attorney Levi Lincoln successfully defended Quock Walker. Under the Massachusetts state constitution, written by John Adams, all men are created equal. The Quock Walker case effectively abolished slavery in Massachusetts. Slaveholders freed the people they enslaved.

Massachusetts became the first state with a court order that denied slavery. By 1790, the federal census recorded no slaves in Massachusetts—slavery had effectively faded away in the Bay State.

Word of the Quock Walker case spread through the South and inspired runaways to seek emancipation in Massachusetts. New Bedford became a hub on the Underground Railroad.[8]

∞

IN 1836, SEVERAL PEOPLE in Edgartown formed a group for the national abolition of slavery. The Northern District Anti-Slavery Society submitted a petition to the Massachusetts legislature, but that august body failed to respond because women were among the signatories. The petition was ignored when it reached the House of Representatives in Washington. Women did not have the right to vote.

Discrimination bonded the nascent women's movement with the abolitionists. Neither Blacks nor women could vote, and thus they lacked a voice in the public square.

THE UNDERGROUND RAILROAD

Illegal and informal are apt descriptors of the Underground Railroad. It was against the law and a makeshift route of safe houses where runaways could safely stay on their journey north.

The term was first used by Thomas Smallwood, a Washington cobbler, who escaped in 1831. The phrase was published in the August 10, 1842 edition of *Tocsin of Liberty*, an abolitionist newspaper in Albany.[9] Smallwood "advised slaveholders bewildered by the disappearance of their enslaved workers to apply at the 'office of the underground railroad' in Washington for information on their lost property."[10]

Frederick Douglass (1818–1895) spoke at the Edgartown Town Hall and the Federated Church in the autumn of 1857. Douglass described escaping enslavement at the age of twenty. He was a renowned orator, speaking across the northern states and England prior to the Civil War.

When Douglass came to Edgartown, editor Edgar Marchant of the *Vineyard Gazette* hoped "the learned lecturer will aim more to enlighten his audience than to excite their prejudice against the South." He recommended Douglass "let peace and concord, and brotherly love, be his watchword."

Douglass's topic at the Edgartown Town Hall addressed unity of the races. Attendees were "a very respectable, though not large, audience." At the Federated Church, however, Douglass drew a full house on the issue of slavery. The *Vineyard Gazette* reviewed both speeches on December 4, 1857, acknowledging that "Mr. D. is entitled to great respect and to the best wishes of all true lovers of the colored race."

Frederick Douglass returned to the Vineyard in 1876 as a friend of Reverend William Jackson. He preached at the Tabernacle.

During his lifetime, Douglass was the most photographed man in the nineteenth century, sitting for more than 150 photographs.

AT HER DEATH IN 1859, Nancy Michael, daughter of Beck, was remembered to have loved children, proving attentive to their wants and needs. She influenced sailors, who adhered to her predictions for an impending expedition. Some considered her a witch. A plaque, accompanied by a Barney Zeitz sculpture, was installed by the African American Trail by the observation deck in Edgartown.

Nancy Michael was the grandmother of William Martin (1830–1907), a Black whaling captain on Martha's Vineyard.

On his first whaling exploit in 1853, Martin signed on the *Europa* as log keeper and first mate. He kept the log again on the *Eunice H. Adams* in 1870. Martin was captain of the *Emma Jane*, the *Golden City* and later the *Eunice H. Adams*. Over more than three decades, Martin earned the respect of his white peers.

In 1857, Martin married Sarah Brown, a Chappaquiddick Wampanoag. Whether by racism or choice, William Martin built his house on Chappaquiddick, rather than North Water Street, among white captains. The Martins had no children but celebrated their fiftieth wedding anniversary in 1907. Shortly thereafter, William Martin passed. The couple is buried in the Chappaquiddick cemetery overlooking Cape Pogue.

PROPERTY RACISM

Property racism was evident in the late nineteenth century. Efforts to grant formerly enslaved people equality during Reconstruction fell to Jim Crow restrictions and prejudice in education, politics, employment and housing.

Enslaved Blacks could not own property and were forbidden to read and write. They worked but were not paid. They were subject to the whims of slaveholders, overseers and the (white) public. They had no rights.

Nancy Michael is recognized by the African American Heritage Trail in Edgartown. The daughter of the enslaved woman Beck, Nancy Michael was the grandmother of the Vineyard's Black whaling captain William Martin. *Sculpture by Barney Zeitz.*

Virtually their only freedom was to celebrate their faith, their religion, their spiritual being.

Reconstruction was intended to improve the lives of the formerly enslaved. It lasted until 1877, when federal troops were removed from the South. Black Codes were instituted to restrict and curtail advancement of Blacks.

Reconstruction was less restrictive on Martha's Vineyard. The Vineyard was not marked by voter discrimination. Rather, the Island expanded voter rolls by giving Native Americans the right to vote in 1871, albeit taking their tribal lands. Still, property was a prerequisite to voting.

We have no indication schools were segregated on the Vineyard. In both religion and education, the Black population was considered equal to whites, on Island, in the nineteenth century. Blacks could buy a house, at least in Oak Bluffs. The workforce included Black men and women. Women worked as domestics, nannies or laundresses. Whaling was the most integrated workplace; Black men were equals yet performed the most arduous tasks.

Less than 10 percent of the Vineyard population in 1860 was Black. On the Vineyard in the late nineteenth century, Blacks were in the servant class, working for white summer people, which would have insulated them from the public.

JACKIE HOLLAND WROTE A defining piece on African Americans on Martha's Vineyard.[11] (See the appendix for the Jones family tree, page 155.)

Holland was the great-granddaughter of PHOEBE BALLOU. Her story adds an intriguing chapter to the saga of Black homeownership. To own property in the late 1800s was a big deal for a woman, a Black woman.

Phoebe Ballou worked as a governess for a white family in The Highlands, the Hatches. She worked "as housekeeper and cook, and was treated like a member of the family."[12]

In the 1880s, she bought a small duplex on Lake Anthony (now Oak Bluffs Harbor). She baked bread and rolls for Call's Market (near Our Market). "Sometimes there were over 50 bread pans, loaded with dough, left to rise overnight to be baked in the morning. Phoebe was a hard-working woman, and her fresh breads were in big demand at Mr. Call's."[13] She was a busy baker.

Phoebe Ballou shared her house with Isaac and Rachel West and their daughter Dorothy.

In 1909, allegedly careless smoking ignited a fire and the house burned. Phoebe Ballou was homeless.

"The disaster set the stage for Phoebe's next move. She bought a neat, white cottage (which had been moved from the Campground) in Bellevue Heights."[14] This house on Pacific Avenue was the family homestead for generations. Phoebe's daughter Caroline and Caroline's husband, Thomas Vreeland Jones, lived there with their children John Wesley and Lois Mailou Jones. John's children, Jacqueline (Jackie Holland) and Robert, and his grandchildren Laurence Holland, Carol Holland-Kocher, Todd Jones, and Stacy Jones-Bevacqua vacationed there.

"Today [1991], the Pacific homestead is still in the Jones family, more than 100 years after Phoebe Ballou's determined efforts. Her descendants all agree, 'the Vineyard is in our blood.'" (And yes, Jackie Holland was the great-granddaughter of Phoebe Mosely Ballou. Jackie's aunt was Lois Mailou, Jones the world-renowned artist.)

One of Phoebe's grandchildren was LOIS MAILOU JONES (1905–1998). As a young girl, Lois summered in Oak Bluffs, sketching and painting watercolors. She was a contemporary of Dorothy West and knew musician

Lois Mailou Jones summered in Oak Bluffs. Working in a variety of mediums, and influenced by various styles, she worked in Haiti, Africa and the States and became a world-renowned American artist. *Courtesy of Olive Tomlinson.*

Harry Burleigh. Her first art exhibit was on the Vineyard when she was seventeen. Her early art included costume design and African masks. She studied at Howard University and taught there as her expertise expanded.

Lois Mailou Jones was dedicated to her artistic career. She wanted to be known simply as an American painter. And her art is recognized and appreciated all over the world. Lois Mailou Jones is buried at the Oak Grove Cemetery in Oak Bluffs.

In contrast to the mainland of America, there was no structural discrimination by real estate brokers, mortgage lenders, insurance companies, lawyers, or the government to deny African Americans access to property on the Vineyard.

—⁂—

3

THE HIGHLANDS

The decades of Reconstruction were a challenging time for Blacks. Formerly enslaved men had no savings, no property, no rights. Women and children had been separated from their families through slave markets. Black people were uprooted from where they had lived. Limited education curtailed their level of expertise as they began their lives anew. Efforts were proposed by civic-minded politicians; unfortunately, many failed. Successes were small but significant.

Congress established the Bureau of Refugees, Freedmen and Abandoned Lands, known as the Freedmen's Bureau, in the waning months of the Lincoln administration. The intent was to provide land and educate the four million Blacks who had been enslaved.

General William Sherman and Secretary of War Edwin Stanton issued Field Order No. 15. The field order was intended to provide a plot of forty acres and a mule to Blacks willing to work the land along the coast of South Carolina. Land was key to getting ahead.

Special Field Order No. 15 fell by the wayside with Lincoln's assassination. The forty thousand Blacks scheduled to assume landownership lost out when President Andrew Johnson overturned the order. The land was returned to the former owners, Confederate rice planters.

Myriad hardships stood in the way of the formerly enslaved. Illiteracy was a handicap. The inability to furnish identification and lack of access to legal services prevented Blacks from purchasing property. Such deficits contributed to a failure to pass property titles to progeny. Without property, how could the formerly enslaved make it?

Greater success was achieved in education.

In March 1865, the Freedmen's Bureau addressed the needs of recently freed Blacks. The intent was to provide education; operate hospitals; legalize marriages; offer employment; and distribute clothing, food, and land to the formerly enslaved. President Lincoln and the Republican Congress sought to meet those needs.

General Oliver Howard oversaw the Freedmen's Bureau. The success of the bureau can be measured by the four thousand free schools and colleges it opened, and the quarter million Black students it educated. The largest of the Historically Black Colleges and Universities (HBCU), Howard University in Washington, D.C., bears the general's name. By 1870, 20 percent of Blacks could read.

Formerly enslaved people achieved moderate success. On the Vineyard, think Isaac West, father of Dorothy West. Consider Charles and Henrietta Shearer, founders of Shearer Cottage. These people and others seized opportunities afforded them and bettered themselves. Others followed. The few Blacks on Martha's Vineyard had begun to expand into a welcoming community by the turn of the century.

IN 1866, ERASTUS CARPENTER and his Oak Bluffs Land and Wharf Company bought seventy-five acres of land adjacent to the Methodist Camp Meeting Association. The Oak Bluffs Land and Wharf Company sold one thousand house lots to prospective homeowners. The intrusion of an adjacent community was perceived as an immediate threat by the Methodists.

Campground leaders had a twofold response to the Oak Bluffs Land and Wharf Company.

Wesleyan Grove erected a seven-foot-high stockade fence around their thirty-acre development, about August 1866. The intent was to ward off residents of the Oak Bluffs Land and Wharf Company, people who enjoyed secular activities. The fence also kept Methodists inside, protected from the Land and Wharf crowd.

The Oak Bluffs Land and Wharf Company built Union Chapel, a nondenominational (if it was Protestant) church on a rise off Kennebec Avenue, consecrated in 1870. It has served as a beacon of hope for a century and a half, hosting both Presidents Clinton and Obama.

Secondly, the Methodist burghers purchased land north of Lake Anthony, a potential escape from the perceived distractions of the

Oak Bluffs Land and Wharf Company. Should the intruders become too arrogant, ignorant or insulting to the reserved, sedate, abstaining, Methodist community, the Methodists would relocate to the land above the lake.

In 1869, Wesleyan Grove purchased The Highlands, a 225-acre landscape of woods and fields, a former sheep pasture. This protective investment shielded the Methodists from the encroaching secular crowd. The hillside oasis was under the auspices of the Vineyard Grove Company yet managed by Wesleyan Grove. The land was accessed at Highland Pier, which already served the Methodists.

As the situation evolved, the Methodists recognized their fears were unwarranted. The Land and Wharf crowd did not impose on the Methodists. Rather the Company mimicked the Campground with a landscape design of graceful avenues, spacious parks and the centerpiece of Ocean Park. Circuit Avenue encircled the community in a two-mile route; a vibrant business section arose adjacent to the Campground. Homeowners mimicked the gingerbread cottages. The Oak Bluffs Land and Wharf Company melded with the style of the Methodist community. Life calmed down in the Campground.

A fence was unnecessary between congenial neighbors. It was dismantled.

Nor was there a need for the protective acreage of The Highlands. In 1875, the Vineyard Grove Company sold the land to the New England Black Baptist Association; it was renamed Wayland Grove. The Highlands, on the hillside north of Lake Anthony, became a Baptist retreat, a religious community comparable in scope, design and purpose to the Methodist Campground.

An impressive wooden structure was raised twenty feet high, with a flagpole reaching sixty feet skyward. This open-air Baptist church, built in 1878, preceded the Methodist tabernacle by a year.

The *Vineyard Gazette* celebrated the new tabernacle: "The dedicatory services at the new Baptist Temple on Vineyard Highlands Sunday morning, were very successful. Despite the unpleasant weather the friends of the Baptist denomination gathered in large numbers, and some two thousand people were present at the opening services, among them eighty prominent divines."[15]

Wayland Grove became a popular Baptist retreat. Houses were built on the streets emanating from the Park like spokes on a wheel. Blacks lived within eyesight of the Baptist Tabernacle. Baptist Temple Park became the centerpiece of the community.

The Baptist Temple was erected in 1878. Over a half century, prominent Baptist ministers preached to thousands. Today the grounds are under the auspices of the East Chop Association. *Courtesy of Martha's Vineyard Magazine.*

Illumination night, initiated in Ocean Park by Erastus Carpenter of the Oak Bluffs Land and Wharf Company in 1869, spread to the Methodist Campground and expanded to Wayland Grove in The Highlands by 1881.

A bulkhead was built across Squash Meadow Pond in 1869, separating Sunset Lake from Lake Anthony. In 1900, a cut to the ocean converted Lake Anthony into Oak Bluffs Harbor.

Wayland Grove, in the Baptist Highlands, had arrived. And thrived.

———

THE LEGACY OF ISAAC WEST deserves a chapter of his own. (See the appendix for the McGrath family tree.)

Born enslaved in Richmond Virginia, Isaac West (1856–?) assisted his mother, who managed a boardinghouse. Besides shining shoes and running messages for guests, young West learned the business of food purchase.

West made his way to Boston, intent on going into fruit and vegetable business. West's fresh fruit market succeeded. His wholesale market advertised, "Imported and Domestic Fruits and Vegetables, Bananas a Specialty." His great-niece Abby McGrath observed, "It was just a little fruit stand. But for a Black man to own a business was a big deal." West added an ice cream parlor, which also succeeded.

Isaac West met and married South Carolinian Rachel Benson (1878–1954), one of eighteen siblings and twenty-two years his junior. Their Brookline Avenue home was near the Museum of Fine Arts. And they had a home on Appian Way in Cambridge.

In the early 1900s, Isaac West purchased a vacation house on Martha's Vineyard. This afforded his extended family a summer social scene in Oak Bluffs. The Wests shared the two-family property with Phoebe Ballou. The house was near where Our Market stands today.

The West-Ballou house burned in 1909. Isaac West and his sister-in-law Carrie Benson bought a cottage on Myrtle Avenue in The Highlands that had been relocated from the Methodist Campground.

Abby McGrath noted that Grampa Benson, her great-grandfather, once preached at the church on Dukes County Avenue by Garvin Avenue. The West family permeates Oak Bluffs.

Abby recalled, "Grandpa Benson, Rachel's father, rehabbed the house. The original house had a pump on the kitchen sink, which pumped the water up from the well. We heated hot water on the stove to take a bath. I would take mine first and then the adults, one after another, all in the same bathwater. Toward the end of the procession, we would often have to add hot water."

The Wests had one child, Dorothy (1907–1998). Like her father, Dorothy was precocious, motivated, self-confident, and extremely talented. Writing was the prism through which Dorothy West reacted to the world around her.

Dorothy West and two cousins were close in age. Jean (Eugena Rickson Jordan) and Helene Benson Johnson were born around 1907 and died about 2000. Helene Johnson's daughter Abby McGrath shared the unusual arrangement between her mother and aunts: "Two of Rachel West's sisters entrusted their daughters to her. They were told they had two mothers: Rachel and their biological mother."

Abby McGrath described her mother (Helene Johnson) and Aunt Dorothy's exploits in the Harlem Renaissance: "When Dorothy and Helene went to New York City for winning the *Opportunity* writing contest, they became friends with other Harlem Renaissance writers. They sublet Zora Neale Hurston's apartment in Harlem and made a home in New York City." The cousins took the apartment without their parents' permission. They "kept rooms at the Y so their parents would not be upset. Living alone in New York City without a chaperone was not considered in good taste, not something GOOD girls would do."[16]

Helene became an accomplished poet. Dorothy excelled with short stories and edited magazines. Dorothy West was befriended by poet Langston Hughes and Zora Neale Huston, author of *Barracoon*. According to Abby, the cousins "are featured in Wallace Thurman's roman à clef *Infants of the Spring*," a novel that satirically paints participants of the Harlem Renaissance.

Dorothy began writing for the *New York Daily News*. Helene worked for a Jewish philanthropic organization. During the Depression, Dorothy was employed by the Works Progress Administration (WPA) and the Federal Writers Project.

Dorothy West returned to her family house in The Highlands to care for her mother. She lived here the rest of her life, publishing two novels, dozens of short stories, and her weekly town column in the *Vineyard Gazette*. *Courtesy of Joyce Dresser.*

Meanwhile, Rachel West and three of her sisters (Carrie Benson, Ella Johnson and Minnie Rickson) made their home on Myrtle Avenue. As they needed more assistance, Dorothy returned to the Vineyard to care for them.

Dorothy's niece spoke of her grandmother Ella Johnson, a nurse. She heard people screaming at the Baptist Tabernacle. A woman was giving birth. Ella ran to help. "She called for a bucket of hot water and a bucket of cold water. She dipped the child back and forth between the two buckets to revive it, a system which is still used today. The child survived."

Dorothy West published her first novel, *The Living Is Easy*, in 1948. The book focuses on her mother's life, a life of luxury due to Isaac West's success with his fruit market at Faneuil Hall; his skill was ripening bananas. Adelaide Cromwell, who met Dorothy picking blueberries, wrote an afterword for the book, concluding that a group who "does not know its history—all of it—is not only in danger of repeating its mistakes" but could also be charged with never having done anything.[17] Dorothy knew her history.

West became a spokesperson, a denizen of The Highlands. Dorothy West used the phrase "Home of My Heart" to describe her love of Martha's Vineyard, Oak Bluffs, The Highlands, and her home on Myrtle Avenue.

In a 1971 interview in the *Vineyard Gazette*, she described the Black community on Martha's Vineyard in the early 1900s: "There were no separate areas. There were too few Black vacationers to form a colony. We were among the first blacks to vacation on Martha's Vineyard. It is not unlikely that the Island, in particular Oak Bluffs, had a larger number of vacationing Blacks than any other section of the country. There were probably twelve cottage owners."

For decades, Dorothy West wrote short stories. She epitomized the town columnist with her inimitable accounts of local events, adding personal details that dramatized the story.

Abby planned to marry a West Coast Irish actor from a blue-color family. She said, "I was becoming a revolutionary, and everyone in The Highlands was very conservative, with Black lawyers and bankers and doctors. I didn't care." Abby married Leonard Rosen, a Jewish man from the Bronx who studied acting and opera. "Had he been upper class, that might have been OK," sniffed Abby. Her second marriage was to Tony McGrath, an Irishman from San Francisco who had a theater company, Off Center Theatre.

Dorothy was livid about the impending nuptials. She wrote a draft of a novel of a mismatched marriage, in both race and social standing. Then she set it aside.

———⊗≈⊗———

IN 1978, FORMER FIRST lady Jacqueline Kennedy Onassis purchased an imposing tract in Gay Head, now bearing its Native American name Aquinnah. Jackie was an editor at Doubleday Books. She read West's column in the *Vineyard Gazette* and reached out. They talked about possible collaboration. Dorothy resurrected the remnants of an unfinished manuscript. Working together proved a success for two historic figures in their waning years.

Abby recalled, "Mrs. O. would come to Dorothy's house one day a week and we would watch her enter Dorothy's house from behind the curtains of my house. One day Mrs. O. left Dorothy's house in tears…. What could Dorothy have said to her that could cause such distress? Evidently, Dorothy was behind in the manuscript and was refusing to do a book tour."

Dorothy West always knew she wanted to be a writer. She and her partner Marion built an adjacent house as a writers' retreat. Today her niece uses it to host Renaissance House. *Courtesy of Joyce Dresser.*

In her landmark novel *The Wedding*, Dorothy West describes the Oval in The Highlands: "A baker's dozen of cottages made a ring around the park. Some were small and plain of façade, others were bigger and handsomer (one, the Coles place, was called a mansion), and all of them were spruced up for summer, set back precisely on immaculate squares of green lawn."[18] Her account continues: "They formed a fortress, a bulwark of colored society. Their occupants could boast that they, or even better their ancestors, had owned a home away from home since the days when a summer hegira was taken by few colored people above the rank of servant."

Abby McGrath, daughter of Harlem Renaissance poet Helene Johnson, organizes the annual community recitation of Frederick Douglass's 1852 speech. *Courtesy of the* MV Times.

The Wedding was published in 1995, nearly fifty years after Dorothy West's first novel. She dedicated the book thus: "In memory of my editor, Jacqueline Kennedy Onassis. Though there was never such a mismatched pair in appearance, we were perfect partners."

Abby McGrath's house, adjacent to her aunt Dorothy's, was built by Dorothy and her partner Marion as a writers' retreat. Today, Abby runs Renaissance House as a retreat for aspiring writers. Renaissance House was named for the Harlem Renaissance. It is designed to offer writers an opportunity for rebirth. She created it in 2000 to give a voice to writers on social issues and justice. The circle is complete. Abby set up Renaissance House as a place to "stare at the walls" and write. She said, "I love Renaissance house. I would sign up for my own program if I could."

Each year Abby invites the public to participate in reading the Frederick Douglass speech "What to the Slave Is the Fourth of July?," first delivered in 1852. It takes place on the Inkwell Beach in Oak Bluffs on the Fourth of July, always a memorable experience.

The legacy of Isaac West lives on through his daughter and great-niece, talented writers, and advocates of the Black community in The Highlands.

The Highlands was the beginning of an African American ecosystem that gave strength and encouragement for later expansion, first to the School Street district in Oak Bluffs, then the Copeland district, near the Inkwell, and ultimately all over the entire Island.

4

BLACKS EXCLUDED

I t's all about the land. Early explorers sought a western route to the Far East. North and South America stood in their way, so they settled for the land instead.

When white settlers "bought" Martha's Vineyard in 1640, they took the land. Thomas Mayhew Jr. recognized that the Vineyard was settled by the Wampanoag Native Americans. He set out to convert them to Christianity, imposing English culture, laws and social norms.

Thomas Mayhew, the progenitor of the colonists, "scrupulously observed Indian land titles, a policy which they enforced upon other settlers throughout the islands and which was generally acceded to by the colonists."[19]

HISTORIAN LLOYD HARE EXPANDS his thesis: "Conversely, it was illegal for anyone to purchase Indian rights without perfecting the English title by a deed derived from the Mayhews." He concludes, "The colonization of the islands by the patentees, like the 'planting' of all American proprietaries, was a pretentious venture in real estate coupled with the feudal privilege of government. The purchase of Indian land titles was not accomplished in one transaction. Tracts of land were purchased in parcels from the native inhabitants over a considerable period of time."[20]

Thomas Mayhew Sr. "protected" the Natives' land. Mayhew authorized himself alone to allow white settlers to negotiate ownership of Native lands.

The Wampanoag denied land could be owned. How could anyone own the landscape? That was inconceivable. White settlers believed their "ownership" preempted the Native perspective that the land was for everyone.

Land. It's all about the land.

———

PEOPLE IN POWER MAY exert control of land for their own purposes. That was true in Seneca Village in New York City. On the West Coast, a similar experience unfolded on Manhattan Beach, California. Both instances relate to the Martha's Vineyard Camp Meeting Association.

Seneca Village became a bustling Manhattan neighborhood. It was founded in 1825 by the New York African Society for Mutual Relief, a group led by abolitionist William Hamilton, an alleged biracial son of Alexander Hamilton.[21] The area was home to "the first significant community of African-American property owners."[22] Seneca Village was a stable, middle-class Black community in uptown New York City.[23]

And then the developers came for their land.

———

WILLA AND CHARLES BRUCE opened Bruce's Beach in 1912 in Los Angeles County, now Manhattan Beach. Bruce's Beach thrived as a popular Black resort from 1912 to 1924. This prime piece of real estate was seized from the Bruce family by Los Angeles County. The county condemned it, took it by eminent domain and awarded the Bruce family $14,500.

A century later, the County of Los Angeles paid Bruce family descendants $20 million for the beach, compensation for the generational wealth the Bruce family could have attained had they operated Bruce's Beach from the 1920s to the 2020s.[24] County supervisor Janice Hahn tweeted, "We have set the precedent and it is the pursuit of justice."[25]

———

THE MARTHA'S VINEYARD CAMP Meeting Association is the pride of the Island. Quaint gingerbread cottages are as ubiquitous as snowflakes yet individually unique. The Campground embraces thirty acres in the heart of Oak Bluffs. Recognized as a National Historic Landmark, the wrought-iron open-air church, the Tabernacle, built in 1879, stands as a sentinel for the noble intentions of the residents of 330 cottages of the Camp Meeting Association.

For decades, indeed more than a century, a secret lay concealed in the archives of the association. Whether by design or accident is immaterial, it happened.

Andrew Patch, former director of the board of the Martha's Vineyard Camp Meeting Association, explored the "outright exclusion of people of color from the MVCMA grounds, which seems to have been at least a somewhat controversial proposition at that time. Enforced segregation of people of color within the grounds of the Association, on the other hand, seems to have been accepted implicitly."[26]

In 2020, Patch, a patent attorney in Washington, D.C., searched through the archives to uncover the old records of the Martha's Vineyard Camp Meeting Association. His motivation was curiosity and perhaps a hint that past activities were not exactly attuned to the goals of John Wesley, who established the Methodist creed in eighteenth-century England.

VIRTUALLY ALL METHODIST TENETS evolved from John Wesley (1703–1790). Wesley preached support of the underprivileged, the poor, the enslaved and the forgotten.

John Wesley was an abolitionist, denigrating the slave trade and human bondage. As a member of the Church of England, he conceived Methodism to expand the reach of the Church.

A young American Black man, Richard Allen, founded the African Methodist Episcopal (AME) Church in 1794 in Philadelphia. He offered an integrated house of worship for Blacks. Absalom Jones became the first Black Episcopal minister in 1804.

Wesley spread the word of God to elicit the holiness of an individual. His theology countered the then current conceit that life was preordained at birth. Wesleyan philosophy promoted the tenet "Love thy neighbor as thyself."

John Wesley was a man of action, riding horseback throughout England, preaching two or three times daily. Over his lifetime, it was estimated Wesley rode 250,000 miles and preached 40,000 sermons.[27]

Wesley advocated for women, often placing them in leadership positions in his religious societies.

Occasionally, preachers were not as erudite as their leader. One preacher did not know the meaning of *austere* and spoke at length of the *oyster* fisherman who dives into the ocean to bring oysters to the surface. A dozen congregants were so moved they converted. When Wesley was confronted by a disconcerted parishioner, he noted the congregation gained a dozen *oysters* after that sermon.

Wesley advocated alcohol abstinence; Methodists were in the forefront of the temperance movement. John Wesley was a force of enlightenment in both England and the states. Author James Kiefer believed, "At the time of his death, he was probably the best known and best loved man in England."[28]

Following Wesley's death, the Methodist Church became distinct from the Church of England.

METHODIST TENETS INSPIRED REVEREND Jeremiah Pease and eight others to pitch tents under the spreading oaks in August 1835. The Martha's Vineyard Camp Meeting Association was born.

For decades, Methodists journeyed from southeastern Massachusetts across Vineyard Sound to the annual religious revival. The flock expanded exponentially, blossoming to more than 250 tents by the 1850s. Black men exhorted. "Father John Wright preached in the Campground in 1856 and raised money for his Ohio college. Henson, the model for Uncle Tom, also spoke before the gathering in 1858."[29] And Frederick Douglass addressed the crowds at the gathering in 1876.

Following the Civil War, segregation spread across the South. Black Codes were instituted, curtailing activity by Blacks. Jim Crow knew no bounds, expanding into northern states. The Camp Meeting Association approved steps to segregate the races. The association marginalized Black cottage owners by voting to relocate and then remove their houses in the Campground.

Andrew Patch researched the saga of Black leaseholders in the Campground in his incisive article in the *Martha's Vineyard Museum Quarterly* titled "The First Cottagers of Color in Oak Bluffs" (August 2021).

Two distinct expulsions occurred in the Methodist Camp Meeting Association. The agent, Judge Edmund Eldridge, presided over the activity, which lasted fifteen years.

To follow the Wamsutta Avenue and Dukes County Avenue purges, Patch traced the relocation of cottage owners and the removal of those cottages as well.

As a result, virtually no Black people owned a cottage in the Campground through most of the twentieth century.

There is a caveat that *may* justify the management of the Association. People who live in the Campground own their homes but not the land. They lease the land from the Association. If the Association chooses not to renew a lease, that is its prerogative. The tenant has no recourse.

THE METHODIST CAMP MEETING Association began to relocate and then remove Black cottages prior to 1900. The Association's agent, Judge Edmund Eldridge, officiated over the removal.

The first mention of segregation in Association minutes was on June 13, 1872, when it was voted "that the question of locating colored people be left with the agent." The agent, Judge Eldridge, determined who could lease each property. Blacks could lease land in a segregated section. Separate but equal was the dictum of the *Plessy v. Ferguson* Supreme Court ruling in 1896. Homeownership, as well as education and transportation, followed suit.

Board minutes from the August 22, 1887 meeting report four white homeowners on Clinton Avenue objected to their Black neighbors. The Board observed it was "improper and illegal to make distinctions among our tenants on the ground of color."

Two years later, that sentiment was challenged when Ezekial Matthews, a cottage owner and town selectman, took umbrage that a Black woman, Martha James, who leased land on Clinton Avenue, sought to open a boardinghouse. The *Martha's Vineyard Herald* noted that Matthews "quite naturally objected to having a colored lodging house next door to him." The Board found another site for Martha James, "in which she is comfortably settled and more satisfied with than the one on the camp ground."[30]

The Association "of course objects to certain businesses in certain locations, whether [for] white or colored people."

The new location for Martha James was on lower Circuit Avenue, likely near the Tivoli Inn. The *Herald* piece noted at least twenty-five lots were leased to Blacks in the Campground. That was 1889.

Segregation infested the Camp Meeting Association.

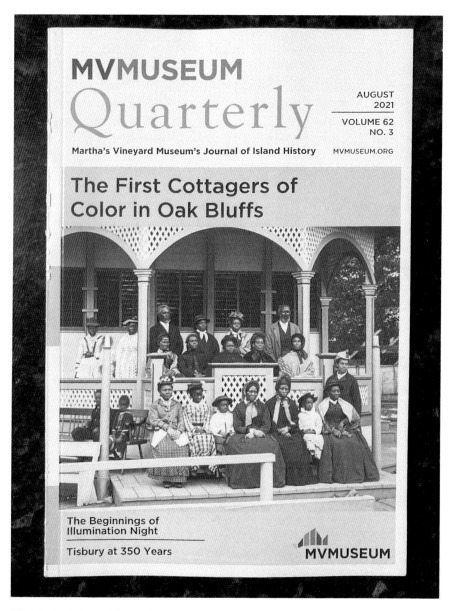

The Martha's Vineyard Museum Quarterly featured the first Black community on the Vineyard, made up of Campground cottage homeowners. *Courtesy of the Martha's Vineyard Museum and Andrew Patch.*

—∞∞∞—

A REPORT BY AGENT Eldridge on October 28, 1904, noted, "The lower portion of our grounds has been given up to the occupation of colored people." He continued, "It will be remembered that a number of years ago a row of these houses were removed from the rear of Clinton Avenue." Said houses, deemed "shanties," were removed for "non-payment and unsightly appearance."

And the houses were all owned by Blacks.

As Andrew Patch observed, "The language of the report is both vivid and revealing, as the defining characteristic of 'these houses,' 'these shanties' and 'those buildings' seems to be nothing intrinsic to the structures themselves, but rather the fact they were owned by people of color."

The relocation of thirty Black-owned Campground cottages took place between 1887 and 1914. It occurred in two adjacent areas, the Wamsutta Avenue section west of Clinton Avenue and the Dukes County Avenue section on the southwest corner of the Campground. (Interestingly, another Wamsutta Avenue runs off Circuit Avenue in the Copeland District.)

The first group of cottages to be moved stood along a street no longer extant, Wamsutta Avenue, which ran parallel and between Clinton Avenue and Dukes County Avenue. From 1892 to 1898, five cottages on the even side of Wamsutta were relocated, still within the bounds of the Campground, yet further from the Tabernacle.

These cottages were moved by August 1895. The agent reported he was "instructed not to renew the lease of the parties now occupying cottages on the East side of Wamsutta Ave." Notes from August 17, 1895, report the agent was "authorized to remove such cottages to localities that in his judgment he may think is best." In short, Eldridge assumed authority to relocate Black owned houses to a different section of the Campground. And this was done "at the expense of the Association."

In his exhaustive research, Andrew Patch includes the names of cottagers whose leases were denied. "By cross-referencing these lease records against federal census records, which do indicate race, it has been possible to determine that nearly all of the Wamsutta cottagers were people of color."[31]

John Ross, a Black, 4 Wamsutta, married Ellen Young, mulatto.
Caroline Becker, 8 Wamsutta, a French Indian, married a
    barber, Martin Becker.

Priscilla Crippen, 10 Wamsutta, Ellen Young Ross's sister, also mulatto.

Jeremiah Smith, 16 Wamsutta, a Black man, and his wife, Eliza, were apparently parents of a Howard University student at their cottage in 1883.

Including brief biographies adds the human element. These were not just houses moved; these were real people, removed from the Camp Meeting Association.

Using Sanborn Fire Insurance maps, with icons of the relocated houses, a picture of the Campground practice is revealed. The Sanborn maps were printed in random years between 1898 and 1914. The maps record significant changes along Wamsutta Avenue during that time.

By 1914, there were no longer any cottages on Wamsutta Avenue. Twelve cottages had been relocated. The street itself disappeared. Wamsutta Avenue became a parking lot for the automobile, coming into its own in the early twentieth century.

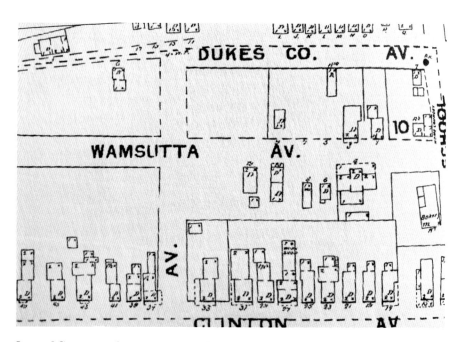

Icons of Campground cottages were used to show relocated cottages. Wamsutta Avenue become a parking lot. *Courtesy of* MV Quarterly *and Andrew Patch.*

The Board meeting of August 23, 1910, recorded no leases for Wamsutta cottages. One Black-owned cottage had been relocated to Dukes County Avenue. That house, built in 1885, was originally situated at 10 Wamsutta Avenue. When the even side of the street was emptied in 1895, the cottage was moved to 15 Wamsutta, where it was enlarged. When Wamsutta itself no longer existed, in 1910, that cottage was moved again. It became 9 Dukes County Avenue.

The house was owned by a Black woman, Harriet Peck. The cottage remained in her family from 1895 to 1978, passing to her daughter, then her niece. It was moved, expanded, and removed again. It still stands on Dukes County Avenue, adjacent to School Street. This exemplifies eighty-plus years of Black homeownership.

A SECOND CLUSTER OF Campground cottages was removed from Dukes County Avenue, near School Street. This southwest area is within the perimeter of the Campground. It is termed the lower section, not only because it often floods but also because it is farthest from the Tabernacle. Many leaseholders along Dukes County Avenue were Black women from the New Bedford area. Altogether, thirty or so cottages made up "the colony of colored people."[32]

The cottages along Dukes County were removed in a similar fashion to the Wamsutta relocation. Based on the Sanborn Insurance maps, we infer the following:

> In 1887, there were eighteen cottages on both sides of Dukes County Avenue.
> In 1898, there were fourteen cottages.
> In 1904, there were nine cottages.
> In 1914, there were two cottages.

Again, the names of those people whose cottages were removed add personal details to the action.

> Cornelia Armstead, 2 Dukes County Avenue, was a Black woman whose father was Charles Amistad, listed in The Fugitive's Gibraltar.

David Robinson, 9 Dukes County Avenue, was a former slave,
married to Mary Ann, born free.

Joseph Lang, 16 Dukes County Avenue, was a Wampanoag/
Black.

Julia Smalley, 19 Dukes County Avenue, was Wampanoag and
mother of Amos Smalley, the only whaleman to harpoon
a great white whale.

Today, there is only the one cottage, at 9 Dukes County Avenue.

Again, Andrew Patch did a masterful job researching the homeowners
who underwent this experience.

Patch summarizes his research defining the practices of the Martha's
Vineyard Camp Meeting Association. It was "to grant leases to persons
of color only for lots located at the extreme north and west limits of
the Association grounds. Thereafter this policy of the MVCMA to keep
people of color marginalized at the fringes of the grounds transitioned

The Harriet Peck house, built in 1885 at 10 Wamsetta, was moved to 15 Wamsetta and later
moved again to its current site near School Street. The house remained in the family nearly
a century. *Courtesy of Joyce Dresser.*

into an outright exclusion of people of color from the Association grounds."

Patch posits that houses owned by Blacks in the Campground prior to 1900 represent the "earliest seasonal community of color on the island." That is significant. He recognizes this population in the early settlement "in many cases overcame unimaginable hardships, and, in the span of a single lifetime, improved their lot in life sufficiently to own modest summer homes on Martha's Vineyard in their later years."

Blacks also had cottages in the northeast corner of the Association, across from the current Nancy's restaurant. Three Black-owned cottages on Central Avenue were in the Campground. Other Black families may have lived nearby.

No. 11 Central Avenue was owned from 1880 to 1895 by Harriet Costello, a Black woman from New Bedford. Marcellus Costello, her husband, was a barber on Circuit Avenue in the summer; he cut hair in New Bedford in the winter. His shop was located near Linda Jean's Restaurant.

No. 12 Central Avenue was rented in 1870 and purchased the next year by a Black minister, Reverend William Jackson, who summered there until his death in 1900. His daughter inherited the cottage and summered there until 1921.

No. 14 Central Avenue was owned by Margaret Prince Matthews. She bought the cottage in 1876 and lived there until she died, in 1895. Margaret Matthews was of mixed Black and Wampanoag descent. Her daughter and grandchildren moved in when her son-in-law passed.

Margaret Matthews's daughter was Eunice Rocker (1849–1911), widowed in 1881. She and her nine children were deemed "chronic paupers" by a local judge.

Antone Rocker (1831–1881), a native of Chile, worked for the Revenue Service. Eunice and Antone married on May 20, 1866. In 1881, he died, and their ninth child was born. Eunice was labeled a pauper by W.B. Wheelwright, Massachusetts agent for the indigent.

Cottage City selectmen Otis Foss, William Davis and Frederick Ripley agreed with Wheelwright's determination, as did Joseph Dias, town treasurer. Dias was proprietor of the Vineyard Grove Home on Siloam Avenue. Foss was a member of the Camp Meeting Association and an overseer of the poor for Cottage City.

Town officials planned to evict Eunice Rocker, although she and her nine children had moved into her mother's home at 14 Central Avenue. In 1883, when the eviction took place, many of her children were quite

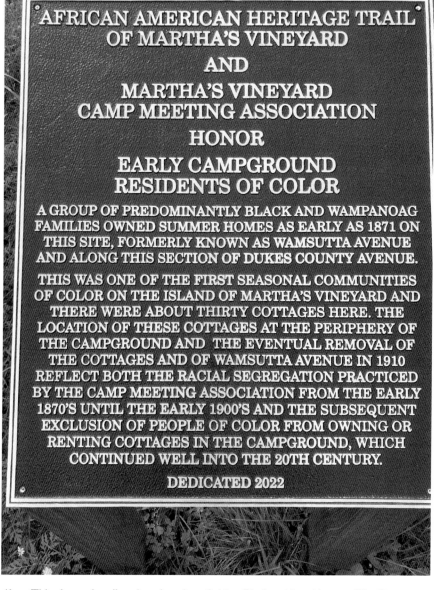

°AFRICAN AMERICAN HERITAGE TRAIL°
OF MARTHA'S VINEYARD
AND
MARTHA'S VINEYARD
CAMP MEETING ASSOCIATION
HONOR
EARLY CAMPGROUND
RESIDENTS OF COLOR

A GROUP OF PREDOMINANTLY BLACK AND WAMPANOAG
FAMILIES OWNED SUMMER HOMES AS EARLY AS 1871 ON
THIS SITE, FORMERLY KNOWN AS WAMSUTTA AVENUE
AND ALONG THIS SECTION OF DUKES COUNTY AVENUE.

THIS WAS ONE OF THE FIRST SEASONAL COMMUNITIES
OF COLOR ON THE ISLAND OF MARTHA'S VINEYARD AND
THERE WERE ABOUT THIRTY COTTAGES HERE. THE
LOCATION OF THESE COTTAGES AT THE PERIPHERY OF
THE CAMPGROUND AND THE EVENTUAL REMOVAL OF
THE COTTAGES AND OF WAMSUTTA AVENUE IN 1910
REFLECT BOTH THE RACIAL SEGREGATION PRACTICED
BY THE CAMP MEETING ASSOCIATION FROM THE EARLY
1870'S UNTIL THE EARLY 1900'S AND THE SUBSEQUENT
EXCLUSION OF PEOPLE OF COLOR FROM OWNING OR
RENTING COTTAGES IN THE CAMPGROUND, WHICH
CONTINUED WELL INTO THE 20TH CENTURY.

DEDICATED 2022

Above: This plaque describes the relocation of thirty Black residents' houses. The Camp Meeting Association paid to move their cottages. *Courtesy of the African American Heritage Trail of Martha's Vineyard.*

Opposite: The Campground cottage residents whose homes were relocated include people who had been enslaved and built a life for themselves in the North. *Courtesy of Joyce Dresser.*

Caroline M. Allen
Cornelia Armstead
Violet Armstead
Caroline E. Becker
Mary A. Bowser
Jane E. Brown
Elizabeth Carter
Lucy A. Cooper
Mary O. Cooper
Harriet A. Costello
Priscilla Crippen
Silas Dix
Keziah Fuller
Mary F. Gainville
James H. Givens
John C. Greene
Nancy C. Greene
Charlotte Augusta Groce
Josephine Hall
Henry Jones

Thomas T. Jones
Mary E. Knox
Joseph Lang
Margaret A. Mann
D. N. Mason
Diana Middleton
Harriet A. Peck
Isabella Pugh
David Robinson
Hannah Harris Webquish Ross
John Ross
Julia A. Smalley
Jeremiah Smith
Ellen E. Vosburgh
Louisa Wadsworth
Dorcas E. Waldron
Harriet A. Watson
Jonathan Watson
Sarah Wentworth
Mary E. Wilkins

young. Cathelina (sixteen), George (fourteen), Frank (twelve), Lawrence (ten), Antone Jr., (eight), William (six), Harry (four), Lottie May (three) and Nellie (one).

On February 2, 1883, in the dead of winter, the three selectmen and local constable Charles Bates arrived to transport Eunice and eight of her children to the Tewksbury Alms House. The family was taken by force.

The cost of transporting the family was borne by Cottage City: two constables accompanied them ($2.50 each per day), steamship and railroad fare ($15.70) and a hack and team of horses ($3.00). "Some sympathetic souls in New Bedford took up their case and were able to get them released from the Tewksbury Alms House within two weeks."[33] For the next few years, the family lived in New Bedford, likely with supporters.

Eunice Rocker sued the Town of Oak Bluffs for the forceful removal of her and her children. In court, in 1888, the case was decided: the removal was illegal and used "improper and unreasonable force in removing the family." She won.

The story was reported by the *Cottage City Star* and the *Vineyard Gazette*. When Eunice Rocker sued for removal, the court supported her. She was awarded $450 in compensation.

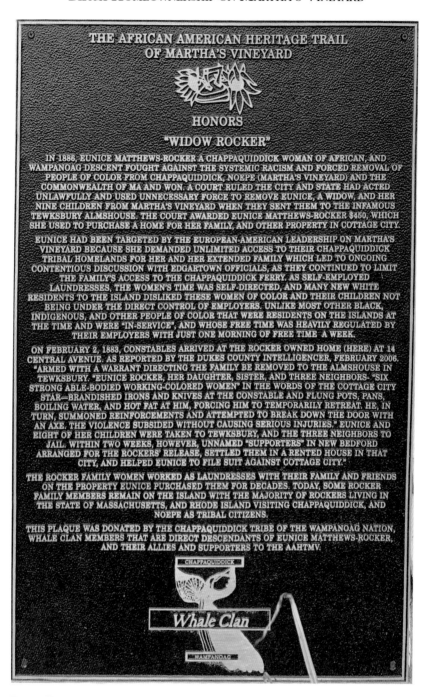

THE AFRICAN AMERICAN HERITAGE TRAIL
OF MARTHA'S VINEYARD

HONORS

"WIDOW ROCKER"

IN 1886, EUNICE MATTHEWS-ROCKER A CHAPPAQUIDDICK WOMAN OF AFRICAN, AND
WAMPANOAG DESCENT FOUGHT AGAINST THE SYSTEMIC RACISM AND FORCED REMOVAL OF
PEOPLE OF COLOR FROM CHAPPAQUIDDICK, NOEPE (MARTHA'S VINEYARD) AND THE
COMMONWEALTH OF MA AND WON. A COURT RULED THE CITY AND STATE HAD ACTED
UNLAWFULLY AND USED UNNECESSARY FORCE TO REMOVE EUNICE, A WIDOW, AND HER
NINE CHILDREN FROM MARTHA'S VINEYARD WHEN THEY SENT THEM TO THE INFAMOUS
TEWKSBURY ALMSHOUSE. THE COURT AWARDED EUNICE MATTHEWS-ROCKER $450, WHICH
SHE USED TO PURCHASE A HOME FOR HER FAMILY, AND OTHER PROPERTY IN COTTAGE CITY.

EUNICE HAD BEEN TARGETED BY THE EUROPEAN-AMERICAN LEADERSHIP ON MARTHA'S
VINEYARD BECAUSE SHE DEMANDED UNLIMITED ACCESS TO THEIR CHAPPAQUIDDICK
TRIBAL HOMELANDS FOR HER AND HER EXTENDED FAMILY WHICH LED TO ONGOING
CONTENTIOUS DISCUSSION WITH EDGARTOWN OFFICIALS, AS THEY CONTINUED TO LIMIT
THE FAMILY'S ACCESS TO THE CHAPPAQUIDDICK FERRY. AS SELF-EMPLOYED
LAUNDRESSES, THE WOMEN'S TIME WAS SELF-DIRECTED, AND MANY NEW WHITE
RESIDENTS TO THE ISLAND DISLIKED THESE WOMEN OF COLOR AND THEIR CHILDREN NOT
BEING UNDER THE DIRECT CONTROL OF EMPLOYERS. UNLIKE MOST OTHER BLACK,
INDIGENOUS, AND OTHER PEOPLE OF COLOR THAT WERE RESIDENTS ON THE ISLANDS AT
THE TIME AND WERE "IN-SERVICE", AND WHOSE FREE TIME WAS HEAVILY REGULATED BY
THEIR EMPLOYERS WITH JUST ONE MORNING OF FREE TIME A WEEK.

ON FEBRUARY 2, 1883, CONSTABLES ARRIVED AT THE ROCKER OWNED HOME (HERE) AT 14
CENTRAL AVENUE. AS REPORTED BY THE DUKES COUNTY INTELLIGENCER, FEBRUARY 2006.
"ARMED WITH A WARRANT DIRECTING THE FAMILY BE REMOVED TO THE ALMSHOUSE IN
TEWKSBURY. "EUNICE ROCKER, HER DAUGHTER, SISTER, AND THREE NEIGHBORS- "SIX
STRONG ABLE-BODIED WORKING-COLORED WOMEN" IN THE WORDS OF THE COTTAGE CITY
STAR—BRANDISHED IRONS AND KNIVES AT THE CONSTABLE AND FLUNG POTS, PANS,
BOILING WATER, AND HOT FAT AT HIM, FORCING HIM TO TEMPORARILY RETREAT. HE, IN
TURN, SUMMONED REINFORCEMENTS AND ATTEMPTED TO BREAK DOWN THE DOOR WITH
AN AXE. THE VIOLENCE SUBSIDED WITHOUT CAUSING SERIOUS INJURIES." EUNICE AND
EIGHT OF HER CHILDREN WERE TAKEN TO TEWKSBURY, AND THE THREE NEIGHBORS TO
JAIL. WITHIN TWO WEEKS, HOWEVER, UNNAMED "SUPPORTERS" IN NEW BEDFORD
ARRANGED FOR THE ROCKERS' RELEASE, SETTLED THEM IN A RENTED HOUSE IN THAT
CITY, AND HELPED EUNICE TO FILE SUIT AGAINST COTTAGE CITY."

THE ROCKER FAMILY WOMEN WORKED AS LAUNDRESSES WITH THEIR FAMILY AND FRIENDS
ON THE PROPERTY EUNICE PURCHASED THEM FOR DECADES. TODAY, SOME ROCKER
FAMILY MEMBERS REMAIN ON THE ISLAND WITH THE MAJORITY OF ROCKERS LIVING IN
THE STATE OF MASSACHUSETTS, AND RHODE ISLAND VISITING CHAPPAQUIDDICK, AND
NOEPE AS TRIBAL CITIZENS.

THIS PLAQUE WAS DONATED BY THE CHAPPAQUIDDICK TRIBE OF THE WAMPANOAG NATION,
WHALE CLAN MEMBERS THAT ARE DIRECT DESCENDANTS OF EUNICE MATTHEWS-ROCKER,
AND THEIR ALLIES AND SUPPORTERS TO THE AAHTMV.

CHAPPAQUIDDICK

Whale Clan

WAMPANOAG

Eunice Rocker was a widowed mother of nine. She was evicted from her mother's cottage and removed to the Tewksbury Alms House in 1883. *Courtesy of the African American Heritage Trail of Martha's Vineyard.*

On September 19, 1888, Eunice Rocker used the $450 to buy a lot and subsequently built a house at the corner of Dukes County and Warwick Avenues, near her mother's house.

Margaret Olivera, a descendant of Eunice Rocker, was gratified to learn her ancestor's name had been cleared and the history of her experience clarified. Margaret noted that her ancestor is buried in the Oak Grove Cemetery, Oak Bluffs. The African American Heritage Trail placed a plaque on Margaret Matthews's house in 2022.

This episode was the nadir, the lowest point, in Black homeownership on Martha's Vineyard.

5

BLACK LEGACY

Blacks were marginalized by the Camp Meeting Association, removed along with their houses. Yet a few determined Blacks purchased property and built homes in Oak Bluffs. Black legacy homeownership on Martha's Vineyard began. These pioneers are to be applauded.

Blacks held property through the years; these include Isaac West, Phoebe (Moseley) Ballou and Charles and Henrietta Shearer. These families established Black legacy home ownership on the Vineyard.

CHARLES SHEARER (1854–1937) WAS born enslaved in Lynchburg, Virginia. (See the appendix for the Shearer family tree.)

Charles met his wife, Henrietta, at Hampton Normal and Agricultural Institute, and both taught in the local schools. Henrietta Merchant (1859–1917) was a free Black woman, never enslaved. The mitochondrial chromosome in Henrietta's descendants indicates she traced her ancestry from a European woman.

The Shearers moved to the Boston area and joined Tremont Temple Baptist Church, one of the first integrated churches. Charles worked in the hospitality business at Young's Hotel and the Parker House. Learning of the Baptist congregation in The Highlands, the Shearers visited Martha's Vineyard in 1891 and attended religious meetings. They bought a house on Moss Avenue in 1895.

Henrietta purchased a larger property, which became the eponymous Shearer Cottage. It is noteworthy that Henrietta, not Charles, signed the deed for the property, on August 28, 1903.

"Cottage City was the only Vineyard town where African Americans were allowed to buy property—provided that property owners were willing to sell it to them. The nearby Methodist Camp Ground was a notable exception, with its restrictive racial covenants," wrote Shelley Christiansen, and "some East Chop properties have archaic deeds to this day, limiting transfers to 'whites of the Protestant faith.'"[34]

The Baptist Highlands was the center of the Black community.

For Black women, the primary means of earning money was to work for white people as a nanny, a maid or a laundress. As an entrepreneurial Black woman, Henrietta Shearer established a laundry in The Highlands. "Skilled at fluting the fancy petticoats of the day, she quickly became the go-to laundress among well-heeled white summer people. Over time, the laundry grew to employ as many as eight women."[35]

Henrietta operated the laundry service in The Highlands so the family could enjoy their summers. Her business was unique, as great-granddaughter Lee Van Allen explains; she had a horse, Dolly, and a wagon to pick up and return laundry. "Henrietta even provided delivery service, which was unheard of on the Island in those days."[36]

The backstory on the horse and buggy service was that Charles Shearer "brought home to his barn a fine racing horse who was going to be destroyed because of an injury. He nursed the horse back to health and named her Dolly. Dolly became a member of the family and a means of transportation to and from Martha's Vineyard. The family and Dolly took two days to reach New Bedford and the ferry to the Island. They always stopped overnight in Brockton to buy new shoes. Dolly, too, had her shoes checked at the blacksmith shop."[37]

Shearer Cottage was one of the earliest homes in The Highlands. "Island historians refer to the cottage as part of an original colony of about twelve black-owned summer homesteads in the Highlands, some predating the Shearers' arrival."[38]

Charles and Henrietta Shearer had three children: Sadie, Lily, and Charles Jr.

"In 1912, Charles and Henrietta Shearer built a twelve-room summer cottage as an inn catering to the Vineyard's emerging market of African American vacationers, who at the time weren't welcome to lodge just anywhere."[39]

Shearer Cottage provided a welcoming atmosphere for Blacks who were refused lodging at white establishments. The inn has been hailed as a centerpiece of the Black community. *Courtesy of Joyce Dresser.*

When Charles corresponded with his alma mater, Hampton Normal and Agricultural Institute, he described his wife's successful laundry business. He noted they recently had opened Shearer Cottage. His alumni letter confirmed the opening of Shearer Cottage as 1912.

The inn worked in conjunction with Henrietta's laundry, which operated in an open-air canopy beside the cottage, known as the "long house," and later converted to guestrooms.

Lee Van Allen described how Shearer is unique: "What makes Shearer stand out is that it was a business, contributing to family income *and* to the community, providing jobs for the Island community and rooms and meals for tourists and visitors. Shearer produced income." And paid taxes. Shearer was part of the economic engine of Oak Bluffs.

Shearer Cottage provided a service to Blacks when other hotels catered only to whites. For years, Shearer hosted multiple generations of guests as well as the Shearer family. Shearer exemplifies what dedication and resilience can do.

Dolly and the carriage picked up guests from the steamship pier at The Highland Wharf. Oak Bluffs itself, and Shearer Cottage in particular, "had

Shearer Cottage guests and employees gathered in 1931. Adam Clayton Powell Jr. stands on the left; Charles Shearer is third from right. Lillian Evanti, world-renowned Black opera singer, leans in on the back row. *Courtesy of Lee Van Allen, historian of the Shearer family.*

swiftly become vacation destinations of choice for African Americans of leisure time and means."[40]

Shearer Cottage: the name conjures a welcoming sentiment and fortuitous settlement of Blacks summering on Martha's Vineyard. Time after time, Black people trace their first memory, their first visit, their first relationship, back to Shearer Cottage. The cottage brought people together. Hopes and dreams were shared. And the Shearers epitomized an extensive legacy of Black homeownership over the years.

LEE VAN ALLEN is the great-granddaughter of Charles and Henrietta Shearer through Lily. She is the historian of the Shearer family, the custodian of the family legacy.

Sadie Shearer, Lee's great-aunt, requested family members preserve her parents' property and the legacy of Shearer Cottage. Sadie issued a directive: "My father and I have always wanted the inn to stay in the family." As Lee emphasized, "The family all worked together to keep Shearer. Shearer was a family business, as well as the core of the Black community in The Highlands." She added, "It is so important for us as a family. It became our credo, keeping the property in the family is what we grew up with."

She explained what Shearer meant to her mother, Doris Pope Jackson: "Shearer is still part of the family. We know we are fortunate. Hold Shearer for the next generation." The power of property knows no bounds. Sadie's wish exemplifies the essence of Black legacy homeownership.

For 130 years, the children, grandchildren, great-grandchildren and great-great-grandchildren of Charles and Henrietta Shearer have held Shearer Cottage. Their presence, their history, their story, filters through The Highlands and, by extension, across the Island. In many ways, Henrietta was the force behind her husband and the founding of Shearer Cottage. When she passed in 1917, the laundry closed. Lee said Henrietta, her great-grandmother, was entrepreneurial and a hard worker: "Shearer is the story of strong Black women who preserved their property."

CHARLES AND HENRIETTA SHEARER left an enduring and memorable legacy to their descendants.

There is pride in this hotel family, responsible for maintaining the standards of past generations. Shearer was *the* place to meet people on the Vineyard.

The dining service was a delight. And when Sadie's sister Lily passed in 1920, Lily's husband, Lincoln Pope Sr., brought their three children—Liz, Doris, and Lincoln Jr.—to summer at the cottage. The pride of Shearer was maintained through the years.

Jo-Ann Walker is Sadie Shearer Washburn's granddaughter.

Jo-Ann Walker has fond memories of her grandmother: "Sadie was amazing. She was so organized. She had everything under control. She did all the shopping for Shearer, and she cooked dinner. My grandmother made sure Shearer was well kept."

There is awe in the granddaughter's words.

Jo-Ann added, "When Nana was working, everyone was working. We all did our best." The women were strong; strong women are what made Shearer.

When she worked at Shearer, Jo-Ann was a chambermaid. "In my early teens, I waited tables one day. It made me crazy. I was out of my comfort zone. I preferred cleaning rooms, as a maid. I got nervous waiting tables."

She continued her confessions: "One time I helped clean up breakfast and had a big plate of pancakes to take home to my family. When I got to our house, they were mostly gone. I remember that!"

Sadie was responsible for dinner and breakfast. Jo-Ann recalled accompanying Sadie to select the turkey for Sunday dinner. "I was young, and the turkey was so big. It's a wonder I can still eat turkey today!" She added, "We have wild turkeys coming by my house now. Maybe they're descendants of the turkey farm I went to with Sadie as a young girl."

Jo-Ann recalled, "Sadie would go to the A&P to choose the vegetables and fruit in bins outside. Once she bought the fruit, then she'd go back to bake the pies. No one can duplicate her pies. Everything was fresh and homemade."

Ten tables were set for Sunday dinner, accommodating forty guests. It was comfortable. Turkey with all the fixings, a fruit cup, Parker House rolls, Jell-O, or sherbet for dessert. A big urn of iced tea sat between the dining room and the kitchen.

Breakfast was codfish cakes with beans, pancakes, bacon, and eggs. Family specialties included baking rolls, bread and fresh fruit pies.

"If they had room for you at dinner or had friends who wanted a meal, you could eat there if there was available space," Jo-Ann said. "It wasn't a public restaurant; it was primarily for Shearer guests." Shearer hosted parties and functions over the years.

Jo-Ann recalled her mother, Miriam, "worked at Shearer a fair amount of time. We lived in Manhattan in the off-season: Sadie, my mother Miriam and me. I was married in 1972, and the reception was at Shearer." Jo-Ann still lives on Martha's Vineyard year-round.

With a smile, she summarized her youthful experience with family: "Working at Shearer was a lot of fun."

In the late 1970s, Doris Pope Jackson, her sister Liz White and cousin Miriam Walker ran Shearer. They converted the twelve guestrooms with shared baths into six efficiency apartments, with private baths. They no longer served meals. As hotels accepted Blacks, Shearer upgraded its accommodations.

Debbie Dixon Toledo (1955–2023) was the great-great-granddaughter of Charles and Henrietta Shearer, through Lily.

As a family, Debbie Dixon noted, the Shearers recognized "that property is the most secure form of wealth. You get wealth through property. Our ancestors saw beauty on the Island. Charles loved the Island. Henrietta was the entrepreneur. She bought more land. She was actually able to buy more land." She continued, "It always was the women. Women really built the wealth."

"Sadie was a spectacular cook," added Debbie, confirming Jo-Ann's memory.

Above: Liz White bought Twin Cottage when she realized its potential as a stage for the Shearer Summer Theatre. *Courtesy of Shera Toledo.*

Opposite: *Othello*, with a Black cast, directed by Liz White. was produced by the Shearer Summer Theatre. *Courtesy of Shera Toledo.*

Debbie's grandmother was Liz White, Lily's daughter. Liz founded the Shearer Summer Theatre and filmed *Othello* with a Black cast. In 1950, Liz White bought Twin Cottage near Shearer; the house presented itself as a massive stage with a huge wraparound porch, an open stage, and met her needs as a theater. Debbie smiled. "That's why she bought the house, for a stage."

Twin Cottage was built in 1873 as a summer cottage, uninsulated, unheated and in a state of disrepair when Debbie inherited it from her parents, Richard and Audrey Dixon. "In her mind's eye, she was thinking of me," said Debbie of her grandmother. Debbie tried to

preserve Twin Cottage, but it was beyond repair. She had it torn down in 2014 and replaced with a modern house.

"[My grandmother] was not going to sell it but keep the land in the family. She wanted the property to pass on, the legacy to continue, even if it was not the same house."

Debbie's daughter Shera is the Shearer's great-great-great-granddaughter, the sixth generation.

Shera Toledo proudly bears the Shearer name. She points out, "In a multi-generational family, we want to hold onto the land. Every generation has held onto it. I don't want to be the one to let it go." Shera Toledo extends the legacy, the essence of legacy homeownership.

Shera, a sixth-generation member of the Shearer family, lives on the acre lot in The Highlands, blocks from Shearer Cottage.

My mother left me with our history, and I am proud to carry on our legacy. I have a new twist to our ownership story now.

6

RACIAL CONFLICTS

As we explore Black legacy homeownership on Martha's Vineyard, we are aware of the mainland, over in America. Although physically removed from national turmoil, national incidents impact life on the Vineyard.

At the height of Jim Crow in the South and segregation in the North, Blacks faced egregious forms of subjugation. Black men were denied the right to vote. Black men and women faced employment limitations, segregation in education and transportation.

A major population shift occurred in the early twentieth century. Blacks left the rural South in great numbers and migrated to the urban North. This Great Migration reflected a seismic shift from an agrarian to an industrial economy, as well as an escape from segregation and lynching in the South.

The Great Migration lasted thirty years, from 1910 to World War II. Six million Blacks moved to northern cities such as New York, Chicago, and Detroit. This major population shift affected politics, society, and culture nationally.

And it was primarily about the land. Blacks wanted a home. Black homeownership was restricted and denied by local governments and state courts, which maintained segregation.

It would be half a century before the Supreme Court issued *Brown v. Board of Education*, overruling *Plessy* in public education. Knowing President Eisenhower and most southern officials opposed the ruling, Chief Justice Earl Warren delayed implementation a year, until May 31, 1955.

"Still, in 1957, Clinton High [east of Nashville, Tennessee] became the first integrated school in the South to graduate a Black student, Bobby Cain (though white students tried to beat him up after the ceremony), and by the fall of 1957 things were close to normal."[41] The review of *A Most Tolerant Little Town* continues: "It's a good story in part because it's typical. What happened in Clinton was a kind of preview of what would happen all across the South during the period."

On Sunday, October 5, 1958, the school was bombed; the perpetrator(s) were never apprehended. No one was injured, but the school was destroyed. Students were bused to another high school.

Desegregation was a challenge that adults did not face. Integration was thrust on the backs of children, white and Black. In the mid-1950s, hotels remained segregated. Buses, waiting rooms, even drinking fountains remained segregated. Clinton High School had no Black teachers, no support for the Black students who integrated the facility. "Desegregation was a war. We sent children off to fight it."[42]

Rosa Parks was arrested in 1955 for sitting in the white section of a bus in Montgomery Alabama. The ensuing bus boycott lasted a year. It addressed the original issue of *Plessy*: a Black man, Homer Plessy, was arrested, in 1892, for sitting in the "white" railroad car in New Orleans, Louisiana.

The era of restrictive regulations, inequality in the workplace, the voting booth, the classroom, and transportation resulted in a segregated society. That affected Black home ownership. It is impressive that Black families managed to purchase property on Martha's Vineyard. And hold onto it.

On the mainland, life for Blacks was much more challenging.

THREE MAJOR RACE RIOTS occurred in the early twentieth century: Springfield, Illinois, in 1908, Chicago in 1919 and Tulsa, Oklahoma, in 1921.

"On February 12, 1809, Abraham Lincoln was born in Kentucky. Exactly 100 years later, journalists, reformers, and scholars meeting in New York City deliberately chose the anniversary of his birth as the starting point for the National Association for the Advancement of Colored People (NAACP)."[43]

The goal was "to promote equality of rights and eradicate caste or race prejudice among citizens of the United States; to advance the interest of colored citizens; to secure for them impartial suffrage; and to increase their opportunities for securing justice in the courts, education for their children, employment according to their ability, and complete equality before the law."

A year earlier, in 1908, a race riot occurred in Springfield, Illinois, when a sheriff transferred a Black prisoner, allegedly accused of murder, for his safety. A white gang burned homes and robbed Black businesses. Most Blacks fled, but eight died. Thousands of dollars of damage were incurred by the Black community.

Journalist William Walling heard white citizens were angered Blacks no longer "knew their place; it was the Blacks' fault there was a riot."

"Black Americans had lost their right to vote and were segregated from white Americans in schools, railroad cars, and public gatherings." The NAACP mission continues to "highlight that the inequalities in American society were systemic rather than the work of a few bad apples, bearing witness until 'the believers in democracy' could no longer remain silent."[44]

Heather Cox Richardson added, "That use of information to rally people to the cause of equality became a hallmark of the NAACP. It challenged racial inequality by calling popular attention to racial atrocities and demanding that officials treat people equally before the law."

"In 1944 the secretary of the NAACP's Montgomery, Alabama, chapter, Rosa Parks, investigated the gang rape of 25-year-old Recy Taylor by six white men." And when President Truman learned Black veteran Isaac Woodard was blinded by police for arguing with a bus driver, Truman created the Committee on Civil Rights to improve "the civil rights of racial and religious minorities in the country."[45]

On Martha's Vineyard, the NAACP chapter was chartered on November 22, 1963, the day President John F. Kennedy was assassinated. It was important to charter the group, even as the country was thrown into crisis and sorrow over the death of the president.

Racial strife overwhelmed Chicago in 1919 engendered by the Great Migration. Blacks moved North to escape racism and seek economic opportunity. Northern whites resented their influx. More than twenty-five riots occurred that summer. Chicago was the worst. The Red Summer meant flowing blood.

Chicago's population more than doubled to 110,000 in 1920. Overcrowding was a factor. Ku Klux Klan threats and lynching added tension. Returning World War I veterans sought equity.

A young Black man, swimming in Lake Michigan on July 27, 1919, drifted into the white-only area. He was stoned by angry whites. Police refused to arrest anyone for his death.

Angry Blacks gathered on the beach. Rumors flowed. Mobs of whites and Blacks attacked each other. For two weeks, chaos reigned.

Finally, the National Guard put down the riot. Nearly forty people were killed, over five hundred injured, and one thousand Blacks were rendered homeless.

DURING RECONSTRUCTION, BLACKS TRIED to avoid segregation and racism. Native Americans lost their land, initially by treaty—later, by force. (On the Vineyard, the same practice occurred, yet without force.) Natives had to abandon their sacred ground; they found themselves homeless.

The two groups bonded and found common ground.

On Martha's Vineyard, the Wampanoag settled on a reservation in Gay Head. This isolated community, made up primarily of Blacks and Indians, survived for generations. (The name Aquinnah replaced Gay Head in 1998.)

In 1871, the town of Gay Head was created. Blacks and Natives intermarried, worked together, and shared the land. Gay Head was isolated by inadequate roads. Residents sailed across Buzzards Bay for food and supplies in New Bedford rather than ride a horse and carriage to Holmes Hole (Tisbury) or Edgartown.

Black men gained suffrage with the Fifteenth Amendment in 1870. To provide equity with Blacks on Island, Wampanoag men were given the franchise, provided they surrender tribal lands to purchase private property. This suspended the Wampanoag reservation. (The land was returned in 1987 when the federal government recognized the Wampanoag tribe.)

In Tulsa, Oklahoma, Blacks and Native Americans bonded on land where they could feel safe. Greenwood, a section of Tulsa, was purchased by a Black landowner, O.W. Gurley, and named for a town in Mississippi. Greenwood became a prosperous, prominent Black community, the most profitable Black area in the country.

TULSA WAS THE SITE of the worst race massacre in American history. Yet the story of Tulsa lay dormant for generations. Participants were ashamed. Politicians were embarrassed it occurred in their community, their state, our country. Tulsa was hidden from history, banished from the public square.

The saga of Tulsa began May 30, 1921, when a young Black man, Richard Rowland, took the elevator to the segregated restroom in the Greenwood section of Tulsa. The elevator operator, a young white woman, accused Rowland of sexual assault. He was arrested; word spread he would be lynched.

Blacks were chased by an armed white mob. Tensions rose as the sun set. Violence ensued. Whites roamed along North Greenwood Avenue, looting shops, burning buildings. An airplane flew low, firing bullets, dropping incendiaries.

Greenwood was under siege.

Over three hundred Blacks died in the massacre. More than eight hundred were injured. Some 1,200 homes were destroyed. Ten thousand people were left homeless.

The Tulsa Race Riot was the most horrific attack of domestic terrorism in American history.

Blacks rebuilt.

———

A CENTURY LATER, 107-YEAR-OLD Viola Fletcher, who witnessed the attacks as a child, testified before Congress: "On May 31, of '21, I went to bed in my family's home in Greenwood," she said. "The neighborhood I fell asleep in that night was rich, not just in terms of wealth, but in culture… and heritage. My family had a beautiful home. We had great neighbors. I had friends to play with. I felt safe. I had everything a child could need. I had a bright future."

She awoke. "I still see Black men being shot, Black bodies lying in the street. I still smell smoke and see fire. I still see Black businesses being burned. I still hear airplanes flying overhead. I hear the screams."[46]

The attack was ignored for nearly a century. Today, the eldest survivor seeks reparations.

"I watched a man with a shotgun blow a neighbor's head from his shoulders, she writes in *Don't Let Them Bury My Story*, a memoir published this year (2023)."[47] The *Washington Post* described Viola Fletcher's battle for reparations: "In the years since the police killing of George Floyd, local governments, civil rights attorneys and activists have embraced the cause of financial redress with a new fervor and ambition: according to activists, there are more than 100 local efforts underway across the country."

"'This is certainly one of the most significant moments in the history of the United States,' said Ron Daniels, who leads the National African American Reparations Commission. Daniels notes that Tulsa, 'one of the most egregious wounds in the history of Black people in this country,' remains a key reparations battleground."

Viola Fletcher lost her first bid for reparations. Her attorney, Damario Solomon-Simmons, a law student under Professor Charles Ogletree, found that the Oklahoma State Supreme Court agreed to accept her case for reparations for the Tulsa riot. "The century-long fight was alive again."[48]

Tulsa was concealed for a century, censoring this violent racial attack.

And on Martha's Vineyard, for over a century no one talked about the Black cottage owners in Oak Bluffs who were relocated until Andrew Patch resurrected the tale from the Campground archives.

———

JAMES HENRY HUBERT (1886–1970) of Sparta, Georgia, was the son of Zacharias Hubert, a community leader who organized a school, a church and a farmers market. Hubert's grandfather Paul was a preacher following enslavement.

James Hubert graduated from Morehouse College in 1910 and subsequently taught economics and sociology at Simmons University in Kentucky. He met and married Mae Bentley.

In 1913, Hubert joined the Urban League. He was asked to relocate to Gay Head.[49] "The Native Americans already had a school, a church and a garden by every house," but Hubert was recruited to supplement these programs.[50]

"These philanthropic organizations were trying to help the Native Americans of Gay Head and Mashpee improve their lives. James Hubert, whose roots were French, Native American, and African American, had the right background for them. Moreover, he came from a family that valued education. He seemed the perfect prospect to assist."[51]

The Huberts moved to Martha's Vineyard in 1914. He was pastor of the Indian Baptist Church, which dates to 1693, and worked with the Gay Head Improvement Association, advocating education, and promoting agriculture with the Wampanoag. Hubert spent three years living in the parsonage of the Baptist church, preaching and teaching.

Phyllis Meras continued: "James Hubert's Vineyard year-round residency was cut short in 1917 when he was asked by the Urban League

Stone House, on Lighthouse Road, Aquinnah, has been in the Hubert family for a century. *Courtesy of Joyce Dresser.*

to return to New York. The League needed his help in planning a housing project in Harlem. First of all, there had to be land for the project. John D. Rockefeller Sr. might have some, he was told. So James Hubert tremulously went to the Rockefeller office. There he was met by the millionaire's architect. Seeing the young African American before him and hearing his request, the architect promptly told James, 'Mr. Rockefeller isn't interested in blacks or Jews.'"

"'I'm not either,' James Hubert remembered replying. 'I didn't come to see you about Negroes, but about land.' That bold reply, which he recounted in a book that is the story of his life, *Profiles of Adventure*, got him the land for the housing project. Other such skillful ventures on behalf of African Americans led him, in time, to become the executive director of the New York office of the Urban League."[52]

Hubert was the first executive director of the New York Urban League, in 1919. The Urban League sought to improve jobs, health, and housing for the Black community. In 1929, Hubert requested "Mrs. Margaret Sanger be invited and urged to establish a Birth Control Clinic somewhere in Harlem accessible to Negro women." He led the Urban League until he retired in 1943.[53]

In 1924, Hubert returned to the Vineyard and purchased Stone House with his brothers Benjamin and Zachary. (Today, four cousins share the property.) He bought seven acres along Lighthouse Road and flouted architectural norms by building Stone Cottage, where his grandson James William Hubert Jr. and James's wife, Jody, summer. (Hubert Sr.'s son Ben earned a penny per stone, which he brought from the Pilot's Landing beach to build Stone Cottage, with walls of uneven height and a shovel jammed in the stone wall.)

Each summer, James Hubert Sr. returned to Gay Head.

During the Harlem Renaissance, he invited artists to Gay Head, where he built a log cabin for them to work. James Hubert also brought Harlem children to his Camp Aquinnah, which predates the town name. By then, his children were old enough to be counselors.

James and Mae (Mary) Hubert had three children:

> Mae Etta Brooks (1916–?) a teacher, her daughter was Sheryl Brooks-Scott
> Dr. James William Hubert (1918–2003), the father of James William Jr. and Jaimie Janice
> Benjamin Hubert (1921–2018), an agent with the IRS

James William Hubert Jr. with his wife, Jody Queen, on the right. His sister Jamie Janice Hubert stands on the left, by their stone cottage. *Courtesy of Thomas Dresser.*

JAMIE JANICE HUBERT, A financial planner, annually vacations on the Vineyard.

James William Hubert Jr., a retired New York Supreme Court judge, and his wife, Jody, a retired college administrator, summer in Stone Cottage. Their son is Jonathan Hubert. Their daughter Andrea Rao is married with daughter Gabriella and another on the way. Gabriella is the fifth generation of Hubert's descendants to summer at Gay Head.

James Hubert's grandchildren treasure the Pilot's Landing shoreline and share memories of their grandfather.

"Passersby on Lighthouse Road have always tended to slow down as the stone house comes into view—standing tall by the roadside—a memorial to the remarkable James Hubert, the idealistic son of a Georgia slave."[54]

7

COURT CASES

Martha's Vineyard is an island. People enjoy swimming in the ocean. Beaches dot the Island, but not all are open to everyone. Town beaches are restricted in West Tisbury and Chilmark. In Aquinnah, a charge is levied to park near Moshup Beach. Down-Island beaches are less restrictive, but it wasn't always so.

Racism was evident. Barbara Townes, born in 1906, summered in The Highlands. She recalled, "They told the people who used Highland Beach that they could not use it anymore. It had been a public beach, but now they were leasing it to a group of people from East Chop. And this was what they told to us: they refused to have any black people on the beach."[55]

In 1931, the East Chop Beach Club leased Highland Beach. Now the beach became private. Blacks and Jews were not members.

Blacks could pay to swim at Pay Beach, by Ocean Park. Or they could use the town beach, with no restrictions, no charges, and a welcoming atmosphere. Town beach is now known as the Inkwell.

Jocelyn Coleman Walton recalled State Beach was called Edgartown Beach. In the 1930s and '40s, Blacks did not feel welcome to swim there. "Blacks who stopped there were told they could only use it if they lived in Edgartown. In the late forties, some visiting lawyers from New York, armed with the knowledge that in 1946 the beach had been designated as a state beach, challenged the status of who could use it." Now Blacks were welcome.[56]

Real estate can be a dry topic. Still, where you hang your hat matters. A house in an impoverished neighborhood often leads to limited public services, poor police protection, inadequate road repairs and weak public education. Where you live matters. When housing options are limited, restricted, or denied, success in school, work, even family life, is curtailed.

Where you live matters.

Systemic racism has restricted Black property ownership over the years.

Historian Heather Cox Richardson opined, "Homeownership is the most important factor in creating generational wealth—that is, wealth that passes from one generation to the next—both because homeownership essentially forces savings as people pay mortgages, and because homes tend to appreciate in value." That is the definition of legacy homeownership.

Real estate appraisers undervalue Black property, simply because the owners are Black. She cited a Black couple who had their house appraised. Then a white couple sat for them; the house was revalued. The appraiser doubled its worth with the white couple. Same house, different couples "selling" it.[57]

Home appraisals are only one disparity between Blacks and whites. The range of amendments, ordinances, covenants, redlining, and blockbusting used to restrict Black homeownership is astounding.

AMENDMENTS

When the Bill of Rights to the Constitution was adopted in 1791, it included a phrase in the Fifth Amendment: the "Takings Clause." The federal government may not take property without paying fairly for it. That is just compensation or *eminent domain*.

Eminent domain was expanded in the Fourteenth Amendment of 1868 to state government. This clause reads: "nor shall any State deprive any person of life, liberty or property, without due process of law."

In 2005, the Supreme Court expanded eminent domain in economic cases, beyond infrastructure improvements of roads, bridges, or schools. The *Kelo v. New London* case widened the Takings Clause and weakened protection of homes. This affects Blacks and minority communities.

Eminent domain was used in the Seneca Village case of Central Park in 1855 and Bruce's Beach case in 1924. It was not relevant in the Martha's Vineyard Camp Meeting Association case, which was a private land lease issue.

Ordinances

"A zoning ordinance is a rule that defines how property in specific geographic zones can be used." Will Kenton expands his definition of zoning. Zoning ordinances were used by local government to regulate who could purchase property in certain areas. It limited Black homeownership. Government restricted home purchasing.[58]

In urban areas where Blacks could buy, public services were limited. Schools were poorly funded. Businesses shied away so there were fewer shops and stores for the community.

In white-only areas, banks refused to lend to Blacks. Several Vineyard towns had unwritten codes that denied Blacks the option for buying houses. No Blacks bought in Edgartown or Chilmark for many years.

Zoning ordinances today are used to limit businesses from operating in a residential area. It is no longer legal for a zoning ordinance to restrict homeownership by race.

Covenants

When municipal ordinances against Black home ownership were illegal, realtors, in conjunction with homeowners, wrote restrictive covenants to forbid Blacks from buying property.

Restrictive covenants were written into the deeds of properties prohibiting conveyance of that property to Black, Asian, Jewish, or other ethnic groups called out in the deed. These covenants were enforced by the courts until 1948, when the U.S. Supreme Court decided that these covenants were unconstitutional in the famous *Shelley v. Kraemer* case. This case set the legal table for the 1954 *Brown v. Board of Education of Topeka* Supreme Court case, destroying the separate but equal doctrine in America.

On the Vineyard these covenants were used to ban Blacks from buying property in the early 1900s in parts of Oak Bluffs, Edgartown, and other Vineyard towns. In covenants on Martha's Vineyard, a given house could be sold only to a person of the so-called white race.

Restrictive covenants are no longer legal. They were used to ban Blacks from buying property in the early 1900s in parts of Oak Bluffs, Edgartown, and other Vineyard towns.

Restrictive covenants are at the Registry of Deeds, in the red-brick Dukes County Courthouse, on Main Street Edgartown.

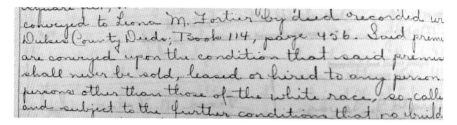

The Dukes County Registry of Deeds houses restrictive covenants from a bygone era. Such restrictions are no longer legal. *Courtesy of Thomas Dresser.*

The exact words of several deeds include restrictive covenants: "Said premises are conveyed upon this condition that said premises shall never be sold, leased or hired to any person or persons other than those of the white race, so-called."

This phrase was copied word for word on each deed with a restriction.

Developer Gerald Savage signed his name on deeds of properties in Katama, Edgartown.

"The restrictive covenant continued to be a volatile matter in the Black community. The inability to rent an apartment or purchase a home for one's family because of racial discrimination was a denial of citizens' rights that could be trumped only by the denial of the right to vote."[59]

It's difficult to earn money to buy a house and get a mortgage approved, but to worry whether a person selling the house refuses to sell, because the buyer is Black, is unconscionable.

Shelley Christiansen, a prominent Vineyard realtor (and writer), responded to questions about restrictive covenants. She said, "I have heard the same or similar reference to covenants from at least one other source."

We spoke with an attorney familiar with Vineyard property titles. On restrictive covenants, attorney Rachel Orr asked rhetorically, "What were they thinking?" She added, "Did they write such deeds so they could pick and choose?"

She spoke of Highland Property Trust, which had restrictive deeds on properties in The Highlands, even among Blacks. They encompassed selective restrictions. Attorney Orr has heard stories about the challenges of property ownership in The Highlands.

She mentioned Gerald Savage, who imposed restrictive covenants on deeds near the hospital in East Chop and Katama, where he developed house lots. Deeds with restrictive language limit who may purchase property.

"Often the deeds refer to a restriction that ONLY a white person may purchase, lease, or hire the property; that usually implied a Christian white person," added Attorney Orr. While it was not illegal at the time, it was discriminatory.

Summing up restrictive covenants, Attorney Orr said, "It was a complicated time, with resort developments not welcoming to Blacks."

And yet, Black families did manage to purchase property on Island.

Jocelyn Coleman Walton recalls a neighbor selling his grandmother's house in The Highlands. He shared a flyer that indicated a realtor refused to sell to Blacks. The neighbor was embarrassed his grandmother held the flyer.

Jocelyn's grandmother could not purchase property from a white man. Manuel Gonsalves, of Portuguese descent, sold Coleman Corners to Luella Coleman.

Racial prejudice and restrictions were present on Martha's Vineyard.

REDLINING

There is no map of Martha's Vineyard with color-coded outlines of which neighborhoods are the best or the worst. That imaginary map is defined as *redlining*. That did happen to the thirty Black families in the Martha's Vineyard Campground.

Redlining is discrimination. Ethnic or racial sections are defined by their value: high or low. A red line encircles the poorest areas. Government services (police, fire, sanitation, education) are limited.

In a redlined area, businesses do not invest. Low-income redlined districts have fewer shops, banks, markets, and gas stations because government and business ignore them. Areas outside redlined districts reap financial rewards and services. It is a systemic means that isolates Black or poor neighborhoods.

Initially, Blacks could lease land from the Methodists. They were, however, segregated to the farthest reaches of the Campground. Today, that is a parking lot. A plaque recognizes the systemic racism of 1900, with names of people affected by this past practice.

BLOCKBUSTING

Blockbusting separated the races, promoted segregation, and fostered discrimination. Blockbusting advocated antagonism.

To bust a block, a realtor persuaded homeowners of a given race to sell below market value in fear that a different ethnic or racial group would invade the neighborhood. The realtor resold to someone in the new group at an inflated price. The neighborhood changed its racial makeup, and the realtor profited.

Blacks were compelled to purchase property in predominantly Black neighborhoods. Black children went to Black schools, with limited supplies. Black parents shopped with higher prices and fewer selections. Black families lived with more crime with poor police protection. It was, and is, a circular tragedy.

There is no blockbusting on Martha's Vineyard. Rather, people of a similar ethnicity choose to live together. Portuguese from the Azores and Cape Verde raised chickens for eggs and meat. They live on Chicken Alley, Vineyard Avenue Oak Bluffs and Lagoon Pond Road in Vineyard Haven, both pockets of Portuguese settlement. By choice.

SUPREME COURT CASES

Two twentieth-century Supreme Court cases expanded Black homeownership.[60]

Private restrictive covenants were anticipated in *Buchanan v. Warley* (1917). On the Vineyard, the homeowner could discriminate; he could sell to a Black person, or not.

Shelley v. Kraemer (1948) outlawed private restrictive covenants. "The Shelley case in 1948, dealing with housing discrimination as noted above, was followed by the landmark Brown case in 1954, dealing with discrimination and education."[61] *Brown* overturned *Plessey v. Ferguson* (1896), which supported separate but equal school systems.

Shelley was more consequential than *Brown v. Board of Education* (1954) in that it created a level field for Blacks. *Shelley v. Kraemer* integrated the races on house sales. Homeownership offers longevity and opportunity. School integration is short-term, a childhood experience. Buy a house where you want, and it can be a life-changing, lifelong experience.[62]

An intriguing addendum to restrictive covenants involves Representative Adam Clayton Powell Jr. In 1960, Powell was hired by John F. Kennedy's presidential campaign against Richard Nixon. In support of Kennedy, "Powell also went around the country with a blown-up replica of a property deed that belonged to Nixon and showed that Nixon had sold his home with a deed including words prohibiting sale of the property to 'a Negro or Jew.' This was a direct violation of the spirit of the Shelley case."[63]

The results of *Buchanan, Shelley* and the Fair Housing Act eliminated much housing discrimination. To buy the house you want offers opportunities, rights, and resources well beyond a roof over your head. These decisions had a national effect on housing options for Blacks.

THE LEGACY OF THE Powell family on Martha's Vineyard began with ADAM CLAYTON POWELL SR., born a month after the Civil War ended in southwestern Virginia. (See the appendix for the Powell family tree.)

His parents, Anthony and Sally Dunning Powell, had been enslaved. Powell attended Wayland Seminary in Washington, which trained Blacks for the ministry; he was ordained in 1892.

Initially settling in Philadelphia, then New Haven, Powell was assigned to Harlem in 1908, at the Abyssinian Baptist Church. Pastor Powell grew his church, in land, structure and membership. His Protestant congregation of ten thousand was the largest in the country. Adam Clayton Powell Sr. was the most prominent Black minister in New York during his tenure.

It was Powell Sr. who encouraged composer, conservator, and performer Harry Burleigh to visit the Vineyard, summering for decades at Shearer Cottage. "The love affair between the Island and Black elected officials began in the early 1900s, when Adam Clayton Powell Sr. visited Shearer Cottage and brought his son Adam Jr. The senior Powell was attracted to the table conversation at Shearer with Booker T. Washington ally William H. Lewis and to the cultural enrichment provided by the likes of Harry Burleigh."[64]

Reverend Powell preached until 1936. Besides the ministry, he was a community activist, founder of the National Urban League and involved in the NAACP. Powell Sr. died in 1953, having prepared his son to follow in the Baptist Church.

Adam Clayton Powell Jr. was born in 1908, the year his father assumed the ministry of the Abyssinian Baptist Church. Shearer Cottage was part of the younger Powell's youth, including a friendship with Dorothy West, another Highlands summer resident.

Growing up in Harlem, Adam Clayton Powell Jr. was a flamboyant beneficiary of his father's prominence. He met a woman charmed by his dramatic persona. Isabel Washington (1908–2007) grew up in Georgia. She moved to New York, performing as a dancer, actress, and showgirl during the Harlem Renaissance. Isabel acted in *St. Louis Blues* with Bessie Smith on Broadway.

Isabel married Preston Webster and had a son, Preston Jr., in 1925.

At the Cotton Club, Isabel met and fell in love with Adam Clayton Powell Jr. Although Powell Sr. strongly objected to the union, Adam and Isabel were married in 1933 at the Abyssinian Baptist Church. Honeymooning at Shearer, Belle reportedly said, "We were New Yorkers, we had to lead the way and set the style."

Ensuring legacy in 1937, the Powells purchased a house on Myrtle Avenue. Bunny Cottage proved a refuge, a respite, from the excitement and racism of the mainland.

Like his father, Powell Jr. became a Baptist minister. He ventured into politics, which dominated his public persona. Elected to the city council in New York in 1941 Powell quickly became a voice for civil rights. He won his first of fifteen terms as the Harlem representative in Congress in 1944.

"After Powell's election to Congress, he and Belle went immediately to the Vineyard. But this visit would be like no other. It was during this visit that he told Belle in their cottage that he was divorcing her and that she would not be going to Washington with him."[65] Belle was blindsided. Author Richard Taylor continued: "No one could match the charisma and leadership of her former husband." She never remarried. "The divorce also marked Powell's departure from the Vineyard."

Powell spent nearly thirty years in Congress. On civil rights, Powell worked closely with Presidents Kennedy and Johnson. He was active in "supporting education programs, a minimum wage bill, the Manpower Development and Training Act, the Anti-Poverty Bill, and other important social legislation."[66] Representative Powell attached language to revenue bills that prohibited racial discrimination. This became known as the Powell Amendment. "He could be loud, he was flamboyant, and he was shrewd and strategic."

For the rest of her life, Belle "hosted family and friends at the Bunny Cottage. She fished in the Vineyard waters and held court on her porch, serving her famous Bloody Mary cocktails, and shared stories of her times

This plaque by the Powell cottage describes the Vineyard connection with Representative Adam Clayton Powell Jr. *Courtesy of Joyce Dresser.*

with Adam, her years in show business, and her years teaching young people in the Harlem Public Schools."[67] A model of the Powell porch was installed at the African American Museum of History and Culture in Washington.

Adam Clayton Powell Jr. suffered two heart attacks and a temporary expulsion from Congress. He lost the 1971 election and died shortly thereafter, on April 4, 1972.

PRESTON POWELL (1925–2022), STEPSON of the representative, was born in Washington, D.C., and grew up in Harlem in the parsonage in the Abyssinian Baptist Church, where his stepfather and stepgrandfather served as ministers. He summered at Bunny Cottage in The Highlands.

Preston served in the navy from 1944 to 1950. "Over 40 years, Preston worked the most volunteer hours of anyone in the state of Maine. He was given the Volunteer of the Year Award in 2004 by the state of Maine, an honor issued by President George Bush. He was an administrator, father, grandfather, and community volunteer."[68]

In 2015, he relocated to Nyack, New York, closer to his son Tommy.

———

THE SAME YEAR ADAM and Isabelle Powell purchased Bunny Cottage in The Highlands, the Baptist Tabernacle was torn down, reported the *Vineyard Gazette* of July 2, 1937. Services had not been held for years. Attendance dropped as summer people spent less time in church and more time on the water or exploring the Vineyard.

In recalling the Tabernacle, the *Gazette* rhapsodized, "Renowned preachers were heard, and echoes of beautiful music heard there are still in the minds of attendants at those annual open-air meetings." Prominent preacher Dr. Gifford was welcomed, and occasionally Methodist ministers joined the Baptists to listen to him.

"Originally the circle in which it now stands had been reserved for the Methodist camp meetings, when it was believed that the Methodists would flee 'over Jordan' to escape the intruding worldliness of the Oak Bluffs development [known as the Oak Bluffs Land and Wharf Company]."

The article continued: "The Baptist Temple was the second of the three places of summer meetings to be erected: Union Chapel was first in 1871, then came the temple in 1877, and the iron tabernacle replaced the old tent of the Methodists in 1879."[69]

———

IN 2023, ARCHAEOLOGY-HISTORY STUDENT Jeffrey Burnett researched the open-air church and "documented and mapped the remnants the Baptist Tabernacle in Wayland Grove, now known as Baptist Temple Park, in The Highlands area of Oak Bluffs. Baptists on the Vineyard held yearly camp meetings at this site from 1875 through the early 1930s."[70]

"In 1877 the Vineyard Baptist Association constructed a wooden, octagonal tabernacle, the main roof of which measured one hundred and twenty feet across and twenty feet high."

Burnett's research indicated the Tabernacle had a flagpole sixty feet above the roof. Construction material had been salvaged from the 1876 Philadelphia Centennial Exposition. The first services were held in 1878.

Part of Burnett's doctoral thesis was to conduct archaeological mapping in Baptist Temple Park, utilizing archival information, oral histories and landscape and archaeological survey to map the construction and growth of an early twentieth-century Black vacationing community in The Highlands and East Chop area of Oak Bluffs.

His project "focuses on the role of space, place, racialization, and collective memory in the construction of this community, in shaping the built and natural landscape, in residents' and visitors' experiences, and the production of meaning and historical knowledge. The events at Baptist Temple Park and the people, groups, and infrastructure that supported them are important to understanding the communities that formed and shaped The Highlands/East Chop area in the late 19th and early 20th century."

Based on the research and writing of Adelaide Cromwell, Skip Finley, Robert Hayden and Richard Taylor, Burnett reported that "during the early 20th century, Black home-and-business-owners formed the core of an infrastructure and landscape that would support the growth of vacationing communities of color. The people who lived in these historic communities, and the descendants and newcomers who live there today, greatly impacted the history, landscape, culture, and future of Oak Bluffs and Martha's Vineyard. These histories and communities are connected to the history of tourism and vacationing in America, the history of Black vacationing, and to the Black Freedom Struggle in the 20th century."

"To better understand, preserve, and share the history of the Baptist Tabernacle, Burnett and local participants, including Sis Carroll, Ifey Ezeoke, Fred Handcock, Steve Hight, Laurie Howick, Maggie Kuypers, Holly Novell, Polly Patterson, Betsy Puchner, Chris Seidel, Henny Skeen, Christie Vanderhoop, and Ed Zephir documented the architectural remnants of the Tabernacle and recorded their location using GPS-mapping equipment."[71]

Burnett concluded, "We hope to discover more about the construction of the Tabernacle, how it was used in the past, and the ways it connects to the wider communities in The Highlands/East Chop area."

8
THE *GREEN BOOK*

n 1912, four white men purchased three thousand acres in Michigan's Manistee National Forest for a Black resort. Midwestern Blacks shared a resort community on Lake Idlewild, the largest Black resort in the country. It thrived into the 1960s.

Blacks enjoyed Idlewild without the racism and segregation prevalent across the country. When prominent Black surgeon Dr. Daniel Hale Williams purchased property in 1915, he put Idlewild on the map. Peers and friends followed. Eventually, he retired and passed there in 1931.

Idlewild, the "Black Eden of Michigan," became a centerpiece of Black property ownership. Prominent Black businessmen and entertainers visited Idlewild, and Black professionals, including Cab Calloway, W.E.B. DuBois, Zora Neale Thurston, and Madame C.J. Walker, purchased property. Idlewild reigned as the most popular midwestern Black resort, hosting summer crowds in the tens of thousands.

Vacationers enjoyed swimming, fishing, and boating on Lake Idlewild. They appreciated horseback riding and hunting in the Manistee National Forest. Evening entertainment ranged from roller skating rinks to bars and clubs.

Singer, songwriter, and band leader Cab Calloway (Harlem's Cotton Club), jazz singer Sarah Vaughan (The Divine One) and jazz trumpeter Louis Armstrong performed, drawing crowds from Detroit and Chicago. Blues guitarist and singer-songwriter B.B. King loved to play at Idlewild and sought to return.

Crowds as large as twenty-five thousand came to see and be seen in the 1950s and early '60s. Vacationers overwhelmed year-rounders but expanded the economic prosperity of Idlewild. Some three hundred Black-owned businesses thrived in Idlewild during these years.

However, the success of the civil rights movement meant Blacks found vacation resorts and entertainment close to home. This was the death knell for Idlewild. It had outlived its purpose.[72]

Compare Oak Bluffs to Idlewild. In the early twentieth century, an amusement park atmosphere sat at the water's edge. Tourists were welcome regardless of race. Blacks enjoyed the charm of the Vineyard. The civil rights movement failed to dampen enthusiasm for Martha's Vineyard; The Highlands did not lose its prominence.

"LEISURE SPACES WERE SOME of the most segregated, racially fraught places in the Jim Crow era."[73] However, a Black community thrived in the Eastville area of Sag Harbor, on the eastern end of Long Island, New York. Blacks built an AME Zion Church in 1839, a likely stop on the Underground Railroad.

Shortly before 1900, Thomas Fortune, editor of the *New York Age*, promoted development of Black resorts. Blacks such as Langston Hughes and Lena Horne vacationed in Sag Harbor. By 1939, plans to develop Sag Harbor were expanded when seventy parcels were purchased to recruit Black families to build summer homes.

This development proved "one of the most enduring Black beachfront communities in America, alongside Highland Beach in Maryland, which was founded in 1893 by Charles Remond Douglass, a son of the abolitionist Frederick Douglass, and Oak Bluffs on Martha's Vineyard in Massachusetts."[74]

In the post–World War II era, middle- and upper-class Blacks sought vacation resorts free from the scourge of racism. A resort subdivision designated by and for Blacks was developed in Sag Harbor. Sag Harbor became one of the few places where Blacks felt safe from systematic oppression. Today, the close-knit town is one of the few remaining Black beachfront communities.

Many Sag Harbor families held their property, passing it to the next generation. "Indeed, the subdivisions provided some of the country's first Black middle-class families a chance to learn how to be rich in a place where their status was both accepted and encouraged."[75]

Today, "Sag Harbor subdivisions are increasingly under threat, as Hamptons developers attempt to buy multiple lots so they can combine them and build outsize homes." Black communities are bought by whites to increase their own wealth.[76]

Sag Harbor, like Seneca Village, offers warnings to the Vineyard's Black community. Don't sell. Hold your property. The Highlands is not threatened by encroaching development like the Hamptons. Nevertheless, The Highlands always faces potential threats of development.

MARTHA'S VINEYARD HAS WELCOMED Black vacationers since the late 1800s.

Following the Civil War, white families vacationed on the Vineyard. They brought their Black servants. This began tourism by Blacks on Martha's Vineyard. Once the Black servant class recognized the peace and beauty of the Vineyard, they wanted a piece of the Island themselves.

Blacks came with a different goal, however. As Anne Morgan wrote, "The surge in vacationers also brought African Americans who came not to play, but to work—as nannies, drivers and cooks." By supporting vacationing whites, Blacks filled a niche in the Island's employment.

Morgan continued, "Soon, this group formed their own subset of the community and started an organization of domestic workers, the Open-Door Club,"[77] which offered a place for Black employees to socialize. Attorney Orr explained: "On the Open-Door Club, the owner of the property made the place welcome for the (Black) servant class who needed a place for socialization."

From 1900 to 1930, Blacks summered on the Island to work. At the same time, middle-class Blacks came to vacation.

Guest houses in Oak Bluffs proliferated to meet an expanding tourist industry. Black guest houses sprouted in the welcoming landscape. The Tivoli Inn opened in 1899. Shearer Cottage opened its doors in 1912, offering a welcoming hostelry for vacationing Blacks.

Realtor Shelley Christiansen noted a couple of guest houses. "Mrs. Anthony Smith ran one guest house on upper Circuit and another nearby on Pocasset Avenue. Dora Hemmings's boarding house on Wayland Avenue in The Highlands was conveniently close to the Shearers, but Mrs. Hemmings, African American herself, reportedly didn't cater to guests of color."[78]

Dunmere Cottage and Villa Rosa catered to a Black populace. Boston Blacks followed friends to the Vineyard, which strengthened bonds both on Island and Boston. This community of equals, of transplanted friends, flourished. Working fathers stayed home, riding the "Daddy Boat" on weekends.

By 1910, the year-round Black population on Martha's Vineyard had reached 193 or 4.2 percent of the total Island population. The Black population shrank to 175 by 1920 yet increased to 295 by 1940, reaching 5.2 percent of the Island populace. In the 1930s, about 30 families were in Oak Bluffs, one of the more populous Black resort communities on the East Coast.

Blacks from Worcester, New Bedford and Springfield vacationed on Martha's Vineyard. Tourists came from Providence. Blacks also visited from New York. "Following rave reviews and word of mouth from two New Yorkers, spiritualist Harry Burleigh and Harlem politician Adam Clayton Powell, New York tourists and vacationers flocked to the Vineyard. Doctors, lawyers, businessmen, teachers, and other civil servants followed."[79] Richard Taylor continues, noting that an integrated society flourished in The Highlands, as "the Vineyard became a place to form friendships, see and be seen, savor the scenic atmosphere and enjoy the beaches."[80]

Many vacationers bought property. Summer people merged with year-rounders, and a solid Black community arose as vacationers lived side by side with the year-round Black population.

A key figure in this merger was Reverend Oscar Denniston, who preached at the Bradley Mission on Masonic Avenue in Oak Bluffs, which had been established to integrate Portuguese immigrants to American life. Denniston's forty years of service brought acceptance and expansion of the Black community.

—⊷⊷—

ONE CAN LINK THE Underground Railroad, an illegal escape route for enslaved Blacks, to the *Negro Green Book* (1936–1967), which listed gas stations, hotels and restaurants that accommodated Black patrons. These two services helped Blacks navigate a segregated society. The Underground Railroad functioned prior to the Civil War; the *Green Book* served Black travelers in the mid-twentieth century.

Racism continued to rage well into the twentieth century. Blacks struggled to find accommodations and meals when they traveled. The *Green Book* met that need in the advent of the automobile travel.

"Postal worker Victor H. Green penned *The Negro Motorist Green-Book* to guide African American travelers to safe, hospitable places, but the subtext was that the threat of violence could mar even the most benign of pursuits: For Black people in America, neither rest nor relaxation would come easily."[81]

Vineyard Gazette columnist Richard Taylor wrote, "The Green Book was published from 1936 to 1967 as a guide during segregation to assist African Americans in identifying businesses that would accept them as customers when they traveled around the country."

Taylor continued: "Recall that Shearer Cottage and the Dunmere Cottage were among several properties on the Vineyard that were listed in the Green Book. Today Kahina Van Dyke owns the newly refurbished Dunmere property as well as Narragansett House. Isabelle's Beach House on Seaview has been added to her portfolio of welcoming accommodations."[82]

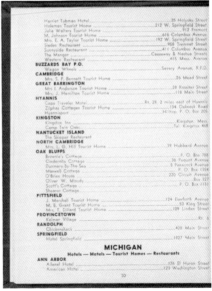

Victor Green's travel guide for hostels and restaurants was an essential tool for Blacks. This 1961 edition lists eight sites in Oak Bluffs. *Courtesy of Martha's Vineyard Museum.*

Local artist/poet Harry Seymour observed, "Richard Taylor's current Oak Bluffs Town Column in the *Gazette* is an excellent historical account of the Green Book chronicling its enormous impact on 'vacationing while Black,' during a period of segregation and Jim Crow. Unfortunately, with integration, the demise of the Green Book was inevitable, as were businesses catering to Black tourism, along with ancillary and related services within the Black community."

He continued: "Vacation spots such as Martha's Vineyard are pulsating with energy and prosperity from an influx of Black vacationers attracted to a place where they are many and not just a few." Seymour concluded, "Ironically, Blacks once forced to be among themselves, now despite options, may choose to do just that, reveling in rich cultural traditions that are every bit American, yet identifiably Black. Indeed, the Green Book is as much American as it is Black history."

Danroy and Angella Henry refurbished their house by the Inkwell. Dragonfly was built in 1874, and the Henrys uncovered a bit of its intriguing past. "We know the house was listed (in the *Green Book*), beginning in 1953 operating as Eastman's by the Sea."

Danroy Henry noted Dragonfly was home to John Ritchie, quartermaster of the Massachusetts Fifty-Fourth all-Black regiment during the Civil War. "It was indeed owned by John Ritchie later in his life. Likely the second owner of our home." Henry added that Ritchie's diary "has been cited as the source of truth for much of the regiment's actions. He appears in the public records in the early 1900's." He said Dragonfly "was listed in *Ebony Magazine* in '65 and '66 and the Green Book for many years around that time."

The Eastmans' granddaughter vacations on the Vineyard. "As we have been jointly uncovering the history, she has searched for and found an

This historic photo of Dunmere Cottage (*left*) indicates it was popular a century ago. The current photo brightens the area. *Courtesy of Martha's Vineyard Museum.*

original guest book." That book may include names of *Green Book* guests who summered on Island.

Today a Black-owned investment company has stepped into vacation resort communities to make properties available to Blacks. "Tracking the Green Book model of looking at historic Black resort communities is Calvin L. Butts, Jr. and Carrington Carter who founded East Chop Capital Fund in 2018 to invest in vacation properties throughout the country. Calvin and Kahina are two talented Oak Bluffs entrepreneurs who understand that land provides the best foundation for access."[83]

ADELAIDE CROMWELL HAD A home in Vineyard Haven. She was a key historian of Black resort communities. She was a sharp, personable woman, dedicated to improving the world.

Abigail Higgins, Adelaide's gardener, shared memories of Cromwell, "a graduate of Smith College, (class of '40) prominent scholar, educator, and writer, and co-founder of the Center for African American studies at Boston University. Although physically tiny, she achieved outsize firsts and accolades amid academic honors."[84] She was a cousin of Senator Edward Brooke.

"Adelaide was always gracious and chatty, which was a treat, because she had so many interesting things to say. She was what would be called a hoot—full of laughter and able to loose a drop-dead punchline, seemingly effortlessly and with sangfroid." Higgins concluded, "Despite advanced age, she was well informed and 'with it,' had traveled widely, and her walls and bookshelves held African art and mementos."

When Cromwell researched Black communities, she recognized a pattern in their composition. The first settlers built a church, which bonded people with a religious foundation and source of spiritual guidance. A school was considered a necessity.

Blacks who relocated to the resort comprised a second group, intent on working for whites as nannies, cooks, launderesses or chauffeurs. On occasion, they found work in an industry—fishing, carpentry, landscaping, painting. The resort was a source of income for those who sought work in a vacation setting.

A third group proved financially viable and vacationed themselves. These middle-class Blacks visited the summer resort and valued it as a vacation site. This pattern was replicated along the East Coast. Top Black

AFRICAN AMERICAN HERITAGE TRAIL
OF MARTHA'S VINEYARD

HONORS THE PROUD LEGACY OF

DUNMERE BY THE SEA

PROVIDING ACCOMMODATION,
SOLACE AND BEACH ACCESS TO
AFRICAN AMERICAN VISITORS FROM 1957-65

FEATURED IN EBONY MAGAZINE 1960-64

AND IN THE 1964 GREEN BOOK

JOSEPH A. MCBRIDE AND CALVIN B. MCBRIDE

"THE BOOK USED BY OUR GRANDPARENTS
TO TRAVEL SAFELY" KAHINA VAN DYKE

Above: One can draw parallels between stations on the Underground Railroad and entries in the *Green Book* a century later. *Courtesy of Thomas Dresser.*

Opposite: Dragonfly is a renovated nineteenth-century house. It was once owned by John Ritchie, quartermaster of the Fifty-Fourth Regiment of Black soldiers in the Civil War. *Courtesy of Joyce Dresser.*

vacation resorts in the early twentieth century included Highland Beach on the Chesapeake, Sag Harbor on Long Island, Cape May, New Jersey, and Oak Bluffs. All sites were first populated by whites, except Highland Beach, founded by Blacks.

Year-round Black laborers sought work first. Once an early Black vacation site began, ambitious Blacks established guest houses for vacationers. The third wave, those wealthy enough to vacation themselves, stayed at guest houses or purchased housing, Black homeownership.

"By the mid-1930s, Oak Bluffs was a heterogeneous black resort with summer visitors coming from all over the country and abroad," wrote Adelaide Cromwell. Her August 1984 piece in the *Dukes County Intelligencer* is a landmark assessment of Black vacationers. Blacks, like whites, gravitate to popular watering spots, today defined as vacation resorts. However, because of segregation, homeownership and rental options were curtailed for Blacks.

Yet in Oak Bluffs, Blacks succeeded in staying in guest houses or buying property.[85]

LUELLA AND RALF COLEMAN summered at Coleman Corners. (See the appendix for the Coleman family tree.)

Jocelyn Coleman Walton titled her memoir: *The Place My Heart Calls Home*, with a subtitle "Stories of a Working Class African American Family…from Boston to Martha's Vineyard."

In her book, Jocelyn Coleman Walton pays tribute to five generations of Colemans who consider their summer compound, Coleman Corners, home. Born in 1939, Jocelyn grew up in Roxbury and graduated from Morgan State College in 1961; she taught mathematics and supervised curriculum and instruction in Maryland and New Jersey schools. In 1993, after thirty-two years in public education, she retired while serving as mathematics supervisor at Plainfield High School.

Jocelyn married Artie Williams in 1963 and had two sons, David, and Kyle. The couple divorced, and Jocelyn remarried in 1983; she and Duncan Walton celebrated nearly forty years of marriage before he passed in 2022.

LUELLA BARNETT COLEMAN (1896–1996), aka Granny, was Jocelyn's grandmother. Luella's mother was Swedish, her father Black. Joseph Barnett was a chauffeur to Joseph P. Kennedy with use of the Kennedy car. In 1908, Luella and her brother Oliver thought it would be fun to climb into the Model T, sitting out front. She had the key and turned on the car. Then twelve-year-old Luella drove around the block and back to the house. Their parents were not happy.

Luella married Ralph Coleman in 1918. Their first child was J. Riche, Jocelyn's father.

Ralph Coleman was a presser in Boston's garment district. When he got involved in the theater, he shortened his name to Ralf. He performed on Broadway in 1933, and from 1935 to 1939 he was the first African American to direct plays in the Federal Theatre project, part of the Works Progress Administration. One of the goals of the WPA during the Depression was to employ theater people and provide entertainment for the common man. Ralf Coleman became known as the Dean of Black theater in Boston.

During her teenage years, Luella befriended Julia Vanderhoop in Boston; Julia invited Luella to Martha's Vineyard. Over the years, Luella summered on the Vineyard, working as a domestic, renting a house in The Highlands.

Luella wanted to purchase property. Often white homeowners refused to sell to Blacks. But in 1944, Manuel Gonsalves sold her three lots in The Highlands for $800. Granny later bought more lots from him across the road in 1955. Coleman Corners was born.

Luella couldn't tell her husband about the purchase because he saw no need for a summer home. "For a few years, she pretended that they were still renting, until one day Ralf asked, 'Why do we keep renting the same house? It always needs repairs.' Ralf was livid when she told him they owned it, but there was nothing he could do about it by then."[86]

Granny made it her mission to bring her five grandchildren to the Vineyard each summer. On the way to the Vineyard, "Granny reminded us that she depended upon us to behave and do our chores. In return, we would have a fun summer filled with blueberry picking, crabbing, and swimming. Without hesitation, we promised. We never doubted her unconditional love for us and her belief in our abilities. We trusted her implicitly as she had never disappointed us. We were a team."[87]

In 1962, Ralf Coleman penned a memorable poem on the Vineyard and the excitement of reaching this placid recreational oasis. A few lines tell the story:

> *The hustle and bustle of making the boat;*
> *When once we are on it, our worries all float*
> *Away with the tide as the Islander blows*
> *For the trip to the Vineyard, and an end to our woes.*[88]

Jocelyn continued: "Granny sacrificed a great deal, every single summer, to give her five grandkids a life beyond the streets of Boston, and she always trusted that we would make her proud. We rarely disappointed her."[89]

"My siblings and I continued to spend every summer on the Vineyard, and as we became teenagers, took on jobs to have spending money." She went on. "Those early teenage years were so carefree. Friendships were made that continue to this day. First loves blossomed and painful breakups happened, and we played and partied together with no sense of class, or color, of the accomplishments or failings of parents."[90]

And there was discrimination, even in Oak Bluffs. Dean Denniston encountered it in the 1930s, getting a job at a market, out of sight from patrons. "Backdoor prejudice," he called it.

JOCELYN'S FATHER, J. RICHE Coleman, wrote a piece that was published in the *Vineyard Gazette* in 1970. He shared his experiences in Oak Bluffs in the 1930s.

> *Being of color was distinctive back in the '30s on the Island. No one saw you. No one heard you. No one knew you. You knew it. You smelled it. But the black did exist on the Island. Even though his natural habitat and haunts were confined to School Street and the Highlands. He was there....*
>
> *White America, you didn't see us. Sorry, Mr. Charley, but your wife's on the beach getting a tan with generations old, tired skin—trying to look like us—brown.*
>
> *Ours was a beautiful generation. H.T. Burleigh, the great organist and composer, with his white hat, cane and patrician pose. Adam Clayton Powell and his wife Isabel. Adam could not have been so beautiful had there not been Isabel. And Dorothy West. She had studied abroad. She had known writers, dancers, actors and all the beautiful people of the arts. She had even lived on the Left Bank.*
>
> *These are beautiful, meaningful people whose only purpose was to create, to give. And you chose not to see them.*

Riche recounted winning a swimming meet but not being declared the winner. Supported by Reverend Oscar Denniston and Judge James Watson, Riche protested to Oak Bluffs officials. They agreed he had won, but the victory was tainted by the tawdry racial discrimination.

Jocelyn's father concluded his piece with a lament that his uncle and father were denied the opportunity to expand their theatrical prowess because of the color of their skin. Once more we are reminded of the unfettered prejudice, segregation, and restriction on Blacks simply because they are Black.[91]

Jocelyn Coleman encountered discrimination in the 1950s; she termed it "subtle segregation." She worked at LaBelle's Restaurant but in the dishroom, invisible to patrons.

Black cottagers swam at the Inkwell. Dorothy West described the origin of the name. "It's true that color played a part, but for just the opposite reason. Some 30 years ago [early 1960s] it was named by the most beautiful group of young, Black teenagers who rejoiced to being colored (which was the descriptive word then) because most of them didn't look colored—or didn't fit the stereotype what Blacks looked like.

They wanted to flaunt or celebrate their origins. Three of them were family members, so I knew firsthand."[92]

From the pride of Dorothy West to the Coleman family, Jocelyn Coleman pulled her memoir together. "Now that I have taken the time to put the pieces together," she wrote, "I feel that I have finally figured it out. 'Coleman Pride' is all about our Granny, Luella Barnett Coleman."[93]

The Coleman siblings in the mid-60s. *Clockwise*: Bo at the top, Marcia, Gretchen, Mom, Stephanie, Jocelyn. Mom was Estelle Rematha Wiggins Coleman. *Courtesy of Jocelyn Coleman Walton,* The Place My Heart Calls Home.

Top: Three generations enjoyed Granny's porch at Coleman Corners: *top, left*: Jelani, Kyle, Elijah; *front*: Jocelyn, Duncan, Caleb. Photograph by Peter Simon, 2016. *Courtesy of Jocelyn Coleman Walton,* The Place My Heart Calls Home.

Bottom: Granny (Luella Coleman), and Jocelyn Coleman Walton, on North Beach, Oak Bluffs, 1940. Granny purchased Coleman Corners; it is still in the family. *Courtesy of Jocelyn Coleman Walton,* The Place My Heart Calls Home.

Luella grasped the larger perspective of the Vineyard as a haven for Blacks. "The Black community on the Island, full of confidence and pride in who we are, has remained determined to maintain this special place, this sanctuary. This is *A Place of Our Own*, as the filmmaker Stanley Nelson titled his 2004 documentary about Oak Bluffs." Jocelyn wrote, "And personally, the Island has continued to be a haven for our family, a place full of good memories, a place where so many people know you, or at least acknowledge you."[94]

At the end of *The Place My Heart Calls Home*, she wrote, "Each summer my children and grandchildren visit, thus becoming the fourth and fifth generations of Colemans to play on the sandy road that is Myrtle Avenue, take walks in the woods, and swim at the Inkwell, just as my grandparents, father, and aunt did so many years ago."[95]

In an article in the *MV Times*, James Dale interviewed Jocelyn Coleman Walton, eliciting the backstory of Coleman Corners and *The Place My Heart Calls Home*. Dale called her writing a second act. When she demurred, he wrote, "Perhaps she's right. She's much more. Jocelyn Coleman Walton is living history." And she is.

Jocelyn concluded,

> *Those of us who represent third, fourth, and fifth generations on this Island have been particularly fortunate because of the vision of our parents and grandparents. We are here because of the legacy they have left us, and we recognize our responsibility to pass on a sense of stewardship to our children and grandchildren, lest the legacy be lost.*[96]

> *Throughout my life, Granny's role-modeling and lessons of "being proud of who I was and doing my best" have helped me hold my head high and take pride in going well beyond doing the minimum that many expected.*[97]

9

THE COTTAGERS

Delilah Pierce recalled the founding of the Cottagers. "It was friends who just got together to enjoy themselves," she began. "Then they decided they weren't really supposed only to enjoy themselves. They were supposed to serve the Island."[98]

Amelia Smith confirmed the giving back to the Island. "One of the original Cottagers was Dorothy West, who told this story of the group's origins: 'My friend Thelma, she told me one day—this is thirty-odd years ago—that she overheard some white people saying that there were all of these rich Black people down there—when they are not—and the white people said that they don't give to charity.' This was taken as a challenge."[99]

Dorothy West summarized their first year. "The Cottagers Club ended its first active season, well pleased with its donations to the Martha's Vineyard Hospital auxiliary and the Martha's Vineyard Hospital as its first charitable ventures."[100] In 1956, the Cottagers was formed by Black female homeowners. They recognized property owners can pursue greater dreams, working as a group. The Cottagers, with their dedication to give back to the community, follow that lead to this day, more than sixty years after the group's founding.

In a 1957 column, Dorothy West complimented the organization for its charitable focus. "The Cottagers Club, a charitable organization now well entrenched in its second active year, held its final meeting of the season at the home of Mrs. Alfred Tynes of Boston, where officers were elected for the summer of '58."[101]

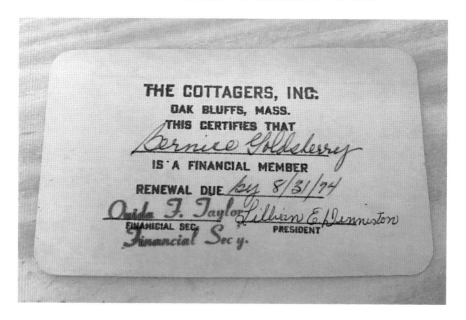

The piece continued: "The new president, Mrs. John Goldsberry of Worcester, succeeds the retiring president, Mrs. James K. Smith of Columbus, Ohio. Mrs. Smith is one of the founders of the Cottagers, and was largely instrumental in steering its growth into a working group, with a serious interest in Island affairs. A rising vote of thanks was given Mrs. Smith in the membership's spontaneous wish to show its appreciation of her fine leadership."

"Mrs. Goldsberry is a clubwoman of several years standing and the Cottagers feel sanguine of the efficacy of their choice. Her acceptance speech pledged her support of their aims and her willingness to give her best efforts to their attainment."

The Cottagers consists of women from off-Island vacationing in their own homes on the Vineyard. "Other officers elected or reelected were: Mrs. Wilmer Lucas of New York as financial secretary; Mrs. Lylburn Downing of Roanoke, Va., as recording secretary, and Mrs. Edward Howard of New York as corresponding secretary."

"With its membership dues, its participation in the Hospital Auxiliary's annual bazaar, and its raffle of an exquisite stole, handmade by one of its members, Mrs. Tynes, the Cottagers' charitable contributions this summer were $480 to the hospital and $75 to the Foote Memorial."

Miss West noted that the final event of the season was "a gay and purely social hour" for the Cottagers and their friends at the seaside home of Dr. and Mrs. Earl Patterson. The piece was signed, *D. West.*

Above: The Cottagers purchased the old town hall for their headquarters in 1968. In 2023, they held a soiree to raise funds to renovate the building. *Courtesy of Joyce Dresser.*

Opposite: Bernice Goldsberry's Cottagers membership card was signed by Lillian Denniston, of another family with multiple generations. Bernice was one of the first presidents of the group. *Courtesy of Carol Goldsberry Turner.*

The first gathering of the Cottagers numbered about a dozen women, with Thelma Garland Smith the first president. Today they number one hundred Black women, all property owners on Island. For more than sixty years, the Cottagers have donated to the Martha's Vineyard Hospital, offered scholarships to high school seniors, and contributed to the NAACP, the Oak Bluffs fire and police departments, the Food Pantry, the Y, the Boys and Girls Club and other nonprofits. Giving back is the motivating force behind the Cottagers.

In 2006, Thelma Hurd, then president of the Cottagers, said, "I love the Vineyard, and when I get here for July and August, I can think of no greater pleasure than to sit on my deck and listen to the birds singing. This is a magical place, and we work hard to preserve this way of life that is so precious to us." She continued, "We want to give back to the community that we value so much."[102]

Amelia Smith observed, "Many of the members have mothers, grandmothers, or aunts who were Cottagers in earlier decades." Current president Olivia Baxter spoke affectionately of the Cottagers: "We have three generations of families working with us, and that gives me great hope for the future that our work will continue."[103]

Elaine Weintraub and Carrie Camillo Tankard founded the African American Heritage Trail in 1995 and added Cottagers Corner, at 57 Pequot Avenue, Oak Bluffs, in 2006, on the group's fiftieth anniversary. Carrie Tankard reflected, "What I like most about the Cottagers is that they work hard and fundraise on the Island and distribute their profits here too."

While fashion shows, which began in the 1960s, and house tours, which started in 1982, were put on hold during the pandemic, "In 2022, the philanthropic group reached into their own pockets to present a $15,000 check to Harbor Homes, Inc., specifically to provide needed furnishings and program support for the newly purchased congregant house for low-income women on New York Avenue."[104]

And the charity continues. "In her 2023 annual letter to members, President Baxter announced an ongoing collaboration between The Cottagers and Harbor Homes, Inc. to continue to work together to secure grants, funds and awards."[105]

The Cottagers established a capital campaign in 2023 to renovate Cottagers Corner. A grand soiree at Featherstone Center for the Arts kicked off the fundraiser. Kharma Finley-Wallace, chair of the Cottagers and organizer of the soiree, radiated enthusiasm. "This has been absolutely amazing and overwhelming, really." She went on: "It really shows the power of support from our community, from our supporters and from our members."[106]

The Cottagers have exceeded their founders' expectations.

The Cottagers lead to the doorstep of Black legacy homeownership: purchasing property and passing it to future family members. Legacy homes are the backbone of property ownership.

As Jackie Holland, Phoebe Ballou's great-granddaughter, noted, "So it is from strong family roots and extended family enrichment handed down by our forebears, that African-Americans have had an active presence on the Vineyard." A common refrain among vacationing Blacks is, "I don't know why, but when I'm on this Island, I seem to be able to laugh and to enjoy being with my friends."[107]

⸺⸺

WHEN ADELAIDE CROMWELL CONDUCTED her research on Black resort communities, she recognized that continuity between generations secures familial holdings, the definition of Black legacy home ownership.

"A legacy property is a real estate asset that has maintained its historical and/or cultural significance over multiple generations. It is a symbolic representation of not only the community for which it serves but also the storied history of family owners that have been responsible for ensuring its transition over time."

Planning is essential. "The most successful multi-generational property owners establish a property succession plan to address both the 'human' and 'property' level dynamics for today, tomorrow and over time."[108]

Families with legacy homes have apparently done just that.

⸺⸺

ESTELLE FITZGERALD BOUGHT A Campground cottage in the late 1920s for $1,500. Because Estelle was Black and the Methodist Campground refused to lease land to Blacks, Estelle had to have her house moved from the Martha's Vineyard Camp Meeting Association. Her cottage was towed across Dukes County Avenue, up School Street and onto Gorham Avenue. And there she summered for many years.

Estelle Fitzgerald's nephew was Herbert Tucker, who married Mary Hill of Philadelphia in 1937. The Tuckers visited Estelle and eventually purchased her house in 1964, keeping it in the family.

In July 2018, the African American Heritage Trail installed its thirtieth plaque on the front of the brick wall of the Dukes County Courthouse on Main Street, Edgartown. The plaque recognized JUDGE HERBERT TUCKER for his efforts to always be fair and just. Words on the plaque quoted Judge Tucker: "While my depositions will have to be fair, they must also reflect a recognition of the wrongs that helped to create these problems." His daughter Gretchen Tucker-Underwood explained that "he always wanted to be the guy who gave the kids a second chance, even when we all thought they didn't deserve it."[109]

As president of the Boston chapter of the NAACP, in 1959, Tucker was asked to file a complaint against the Boston Red Sox with the Massachusetts Commission Against Discrimination. That compelled the Red Sox to integrate their team. In July 1959, Pumpsie Green was signed by the Red Sox, the last professional baseball team to integrate.

Daughter Gretchen recalled, "And there were certain beaches we were not allowed to go to because Boston was so segregated and so evil about public access to beaches. And so my father, he integrated this beach in South Boston, and it was a big deal—how they walked on the beach." Gretchen was too young to grasp the significance of integrating the beach at the time. Today, she recognizes his bravery and determination to integrate a public beach.[110]

Left: Gretchen Tucker Underwood lives in the house of her great-aunt Estelle Fitzgerald. *Courtesy of Joyce Dresser.*

Below: Gretchen Tucker Underwood's house is a former Campground cottage, relocated by the Camp Meeting Association. *Courtesy of Joyce Dresser.*

Opposite: An early photo of Estelle Fitzgerald's house, removed about 1930. *Courtesy of Gretchen Tucker Underwood.*

Tucker founded the first Black law firm in Boston, Cardozo and Tucker. Herbert Tucker worked on the Senate and presidential campaigns of John F. Kennedy. And he was appointed assistant attorney general under Attorney General Edward Brooke.

Judge Tucker (1915–2007) presided over the Edgartown district court from 1979 to 1985.

Gretchen Underwood's daughter, Gretchen Mercer, said of her late grandfather that he was a "huge grizzly bear on the outside, but an absolute teddy bear on the inside."[111]

The earliest photo of Herbert Tucker on the Vineyard is dated 1925. The Tuckers moved to Oak Bluffs in 1960. On Island, Tucker was "just as comfortable at the Inkwell as he was at the East Chop Beach Club." (They were the second Black couple to join the Club. Dr. Cornelius Garland, founder of Plymouth Hospital in Boston, was the first Black invited to join the East Chop Beach Club. He was the father of Thelma Garland Smith, the first president of the Cottagers.) He and his wife, Mary, were longtime members of Grace Episcopal Church in Vineyard Haven.[112]

"When the Reverend John Melville Burgess became the 12th bishop of the Episcopal Diocese of Massachusetts, making him the first African American diocesan bishop of the church in the U.S., it was Mary who worked to have two stained glass windows created and put in Grace Church commemorating Burgess and his work." The first window honored Bishop Burgess; the second was dedicated to Absalom Jones, the first Black Episcopal priest. The stained-glass windows were installed at Grace Church in 1999 in recognition of Bishop Burgess's ninetieth birthday.[113]

Mary Tucker is credited with establishing the popular summer lobster roll program at Grace Church, beginning in 1990, still going strong thirty years on.

As a registered nurse, Mary Tucker (1918–2021) "was a good listener, and tolerant of all kinds of things. She would always tell me, 'Be patient, be loving,'" Tucker Underwood said. She added, "My mother's parents, both of them, were children of slaves. The fact that they were college-educated, and she was college-educated, and my sister and I were educated, she was always so proud. She knew we would always carry that on."

Mary Tucker was a talented tennis player. She hosted a tennis invitational at the Gorham Street court for nearly four decades. The tournament included tennis players from around the world. It was mixed doubles, with partners assigned rather than chosen. "You could be a social professional, and instead of getting paired with another experienced player, you get paired with a 10-year-old—it made for fun tennis, that's for sure," Tucker Underwood said—"a tennis family," as she put it. Of her mother, she added, "She never missed a match, and when she couldn't play, she would sit and watch."

The Tuckers had two daughters, Gwendolyn and Gretchen. GWENDOLYN HILL WHARTON had one son, Richard G. Wharton. For thirty years, she worked on the Metro pages of the *Boston Globe*. Gwen was an enthusiastic dancer and a dedicated gardener. She passed in 2011.

GRETCHEN TUCKER UNDERWOOD taught at Brookline High School, rising to dean of students. She retired after a forty-year commitment. She has one daughter, Gretchen Mercer. Her daughter has two sons: Jason Mercer and Brandon Mercer. Jason has a daughter, Kay Nova Mercer, born in 2023. Kay is the sixth generation of the same family to stay in the same house on Martha's Vineyard.

"Speaking of powerful voices and history, Gretchen Tucker Underwood is following in the footsteps of her late father, Judge Herbert Tucker, and her amazing mother Mary Tucker. She was pleasantly surprised when she received a phone call from State Rep. Dylan Fernandes, who had nominated her for recognition by the Commission on the Status of Women in the Commonwealth."

"The nomination was accompanied by a handful of citations—one citation was from Speaker of the House of Representatives Robert DeLeo recognizing her as the 2019 Unsung Heroine Award for 'unwavering dedication to the community of Martha's Vineyard,' and another came from Governor Charlie Baker, also praising her work here on the Island. If that was not enough, she also was recognized with a Certificate of Merit by the Vineyard Branch of the NAACP."[114]

Gretchen enjoys the comforts of an expanded Campground cottage not far from Sunset Lake in Oak Bluffs. While she appreciates the proximity of her house to downtown, she's aware why her house is where it is.

Gretchen; her parents, Judge Herbert and Mary Tucker, and great-aunt Estelle; her children; grandchildren; and great-grandchildren represent six generations, a living embodiment of Black legacy homeownership on Martha's Vineyard.

In 2023, Navigator Homes will be a site for senior living. Of the five pods in Navigator Homes, one may be named in honor of Judge Herbert and Mary Tucker, a fitting recognition of their dedication to Martha's Vineyard.

JULIA BURGESS TRACES FOUR generations of her family owning property in Vineyard Haven. Her parents, BISHOP JOHN BURGESS and ESTHER BURGESS, first visited the Island in the 1950s along with their daughters, Julia and Margaret. They were guests of Frank and Harriet Sayre. Beginning in the early '60s, Bishop Burgess served as a pastor of summer services at the Chilmark Community Center. The Episcopal Church provided the family with housing each summer, in Chilmark and Vineyard Haven.

In 1970, Bishop Burgess bought a house on Pine Street Vineyard Haven, still in the family. It is in an enclave with other Black families and a short walk to the steamship. The family continues to summer on the Vineyard. Keith and Betty Rawlins were close friends. The friendship between the Burgesses and Judge Herbert and Mary Tucker also blossomed over the years and flowered when the Burgesses retired on Island year-round in 1989.

The Burgesses, Rawlins and Tuckers were members of Grace Episcopal Church. A stained-glass window in honor of Bishop Burgess was installed on his ninetieth birthday in 1999.

John Burgess was born in Michigan in 1909. The *Vineyard Gazette* defined him as "among the last of the Episcopal Church's great progressive bishops of the 20th century."[115] He made a concerted effort to include racial minorities and the urban poor in his ministry.

In 1945, Bishop married Esther Taylor, an activist like her husband. In 1964, at the Ponce De Leon Motel in St. Augustine, Florida, Esther was arrested for refusing to leave the Motel after she was told she could not eat in the dining room; she would have to eat in the kitchen. Her participation in this civil rights protest lives on today.

For a decade, Bishop Burgess served as the first denominational chaplain at Howard University, which included running a center for mostly African

Above: The Grace Episcopal Church in Vineyard Haven showcases stained-glass windows featuring Absalom Jones and Bishop John Burgess. *Courtesy of Julia Burgess.*

Opposite: Bishop John Burgess was the first Black bishop in the Episcopal Church. *Courtesy of Julia Burgess.*

Esther Burgess, Granny, surrounded by her loving family. *Courtesy of Julia Burgess.*

and West Indian students. He was the first African American to serve as a canon at the Washington National Cathedral. Always an advocate for positive social change, Bishop Burgess became an active participant in developing a religious mission to involve churches in improving the lives of the urban poor in the Washington D.C. community.

He was elected suffragan bishop in the Episcopal Diocese of Massachusetts in 1962. In 1969, he was elected bishop, thus becoming the first Black minister to lead a diocese. Bishop Burgess served from 1970 until his retirement five years later. In retirement, Bishop Burgess "served as a hospice visitor and enjoyed volunteering as a reader to schoolchildren on the Vineyard."

John and Esther Bishop had two daughters, Julia and Margaret. Julia Burgess has a daughter, Yvonne Williams, and a son, Kevin Williams, and three grandchildren: Damonte, Ajaun, and Kendall. Julia was executive director of Martha's Vineyard Community Services from 2006 to 2013.

Her sister, Margaret Harrison, has a daughter, Lisa, married to Reggie Joyner, and grandchildren Hewitt and Alysse. Their house is adjacent to Julia's on Midland Street.

Julia Burgess mentioned the impressive reading at the Vineyard Playhouse of Kathy McGhee's play *Miss Maybelline's Nocturnal Flights of Fancy* enacted by Tony-nominated actress S. Epatha Merkerson. McGhee's house was one of those relocated from the Campground in the late 1800s.

BARBARA EDELIN SHARED HER Black legacy story:

My grandmother, Sallie Fisher Clark (1889–1957), an educator from Washington, DC, bought two houses on Waban Park around 1947, "on her way home one day from the store," according to family folklore! The houses are directly across from each other at 18 Pennacook (the back of this house sits on Tuckernuck on Waban Park) and 18 Nantucket.[116]

My grandmother, who was a single mother, having lost my grandfather, Harold Clark, to pneumonia, shortly after the birth of my mother and her twin brother Harold, was able to keep both houses in the family until her death in 1957. Upon her death, the houses passed to my mother Harriette and her brother Harold, but the expenses were difficult for a stay-at-home mom and a Navy officer. It was decided

Left: The historic Clark/Evans house on Nantucket Avenue overlooks Waban Park and the Inkwell, on what was known as the gold coast. *Courtesy of Barbara Edelin.*

Below: The Clark/Evans house today is shared among three sisters, a legacy that began with their grandmother. *Courtesy of Joyce Dresser.*

to keep the smaller house on Nantucket and give the larger house on Pennacook to my mother's first cousin, Charles Fisher. He left his house to his two children, Charles (a year-round Vineyarder) and Kendall a successful lawyer.

My mother passed in February 2020 and left the house on Nantucket to my two sisters, Lesley Christian, Harriette Smith, and me. We continue to enjoy the legacy our grandmother gave us with our own children and grandchildren. We consider it HOME.[117]

10

FAIR HOUSING

E dward W. Brooke was not a legacy homeowner on Martha's Vineyard. However, he contributed major influences on Black homeownership. As a sitting U.S. senator, he vacationed in Oak Bluffs. And he led legislation to expand fair housing opportunities for Blacks.

In 2023, the *Boston Globe* noted the political influence of Blacks on the Vineyard. "Before the civil rights movement, Black Americans were denied access to pools, beaches, and resorts in much of the country, but Oak Bluffs was a welcome exception, including the historic Inkwell Beach. The Black summer community on the island continuously grew, as did its prominence."

The piece continued:

> *Frederick Douglass, the former slave, storied author, and abolitionist, spoke at the Federated Church in Edgartown in 1857. The island has also hosted luminaries like writer Maya Angelou and Harlem Renaissance author Dorothy West. Martin Luther King Jr., who frequented the island in the summer, stayed at the Overton House, an inn in Oak Bluffs. The island was seasonally home to Edward W. Brooke, the first Black senator after Reconstruction, presidential advisers Valerie Jarrett and Vernon Jordan, and Harvard professors Henry Louis Gates Jr. and Charles J. Ogletree Jr., who died earlier this summer.*[118]

When Senator Edward W. Brooke stepped onto center stage in the late 1960s, he continued a dynamic career for equal treatment of all citizens.

As Congress convened on January 10, 1967, Senator Brooke was welcomed to the upper chamber as the first publicly elected Black man to the Senate. At the same time, Representative Adam Clayton Powell Jr., "the most powerful Black man in American political history was in trouble." Powell's brash style brought charges of defamation, extravagant spending, and misappropriation of federal funds. "Two sons of Martha's Vineyard wielded unparalleled political power during a transformative time in American history."[119]

Edward William Brooke (1919–2015) was born in Washington during the Roaring Twenties, amid Prohibition and female suffrage. He recalled, "I grew up black in the segregated South, yet I never knew the poverty or overt racial discrimination that might suggest." He went on, "I attended good schools and lived in a neighborhood that was attractive and crime-free. My life was dramatically different from that of a young black man in the Deep South."[120] Brooke's grandfather had been born enslaved in Fredericksburg, Virginia.

Brooke's family was middle-class Episcopalian and vacationed on Highland Beach, Maryland. In politics, he reflected, "My father was a Republican, as almost all Negroes were then; they rallied around the party of Lincoln and Emancipation." As the Depression deepened, his family appreciated the policies of President Franklin Roosevelt, a Democrat.

Brooke graduated from Dunbar High School in 1936 with plans to become a doctor because he liked the prestige and beautiful women he associated with physicians. Failing his chemistry class at Howard compelled him to revise his career path. "I was more concerned with my social life than chemistry. I had no great urge to be a doctor."

Brooke's father bought his first car in 1938, a shiny new Buick. Because his father never learned to drive, Ed became the family chauffeur and enjoyed use of the car.

When the Daughters of the American Revolution refused to allow Marian Anderson to perform at Constitution Hall because she was Black, Ed and his mother attended the free concert Miss Anderson gave at the Lincoln Memorial, orchestrated by Eleanor Roosevelt. They loved it.

The family purchased their first house in 1941. Ed graduated from Howard, and in December, following Pearl Harbor, he enlisted.

Brooke earned the rank of captain in the segregated 366th Infantry Regiment. Stationed in Italy in 1945, he fell in love with Remigia Ferrari

Scacco. They were married in 1947 and became parents of daughters Remi and Edwina. The next step was to buy a house.

"And that's when the decorated veteran, who fought so arduously for his country, experienced firsthand the discrimination the Black community faced when it came to purchasing real estate." Denied purchase of the property he wanted because he was Black, Edward W. Brooke forged a career based on equal treatment of *all* citizens.[121]

He earned his law degree at Boston University Law School in 1948 and spent a decade practicing law. His anguish over poor and Black families facing challenges in homeownership was ever-present.

Brooke vacationed on Martha's Vineyard from the 1950s until he passed in 2014. He purchased property not far from the Inkwell. During his years on the Vineyard, Brooke taught children to swim at the Inkwell and was active in local social circles. Children and adults knew him as "Uncle Ed"; his ubiquitous smile was welcome everywhere.

Brooke attempted to establish a Black social club in Oak Bluffs in the late 1950s, as Blacks were unwelcome at the local beach, golf, and tennis clubs. His request was denied. Socialization occurred in private homes, on the beach or at Brooke's home.

He bought the house behind his, on Nashawena Avenue, and connected the two, inviting his widowed mother, Helen, a longtime Cottager, to live with his family yet in her own home. His house bears a plaque from the African American Heritage Trail of Martha's Vineyard.

Brooke ventured into Massachusetts politics. He won his 1962 campaign to become the first Black elected attorney general, reelected in 1964. Using

Marie Allen was a longtime Oak Bluffs resident. This flyer was on the fence of her house when she passed in 2023. *Courtesy of Thomas Dresser.*

that position to run for the Senate, Edward W. Brooke III became the first popularly elected Black man to reach the U.S. Senate, in 1967. He won a second term in 1973 as a Republican, serving until 1979.

Senator Edward W. Brooke assumed leadership to expand fair housing. "During his time in Senate, Brooke developed a deep passion for addressing housing issues. In collaboration with Minnesota Senator Walter Mondale, he co-sponsored the Fair Housing Act of 1968." This was a key element of the 1968 Civil Rights Act.[122]

"Brooke was a champion and lead protagonist of the Civil Rights Act of 1968, which prohibited discrimination in the sale, rental, and financing of housing, based on race, religion, or national origin. Title VIII of the act became known as the Fair Housing Act of 1968. Johnson signed the act on April 11, just a week after King's death."[123]

Senator Brooke made homeownership possible for people with low incomes without regard to race. That was a major shift in the national perspective, as property was integral to the right to vote. By working for the impoverished, Brooke expanded opportunity for everyone.

Fairness and independence were hallmarks of Edward W. Brooke. He became an ambassador, a troubadour for Martha's Vineyard, encouraging Blacks to visit and purchase property. He was not the first ambassador, nor the last, but his contributions to Island life, especially for the Black community, live on. "[Representative Adam Clayton] Powell and Brooke shared an unmatched love of Martha's Vineyard, became active participants in national politics at the highest levels, and fought for justice and fairness for all our nation."[124]

Senator Brooke was presented with the Presidential Medal of Freedom by President George W. Bush in 2004; five years later, he was awarded the Congressional Gold Medal. *Bridging the Divide: My Life* was published in 2006. In his autobiography, Brooke shared his views on race as a Black Republican in Massachusetts, a liberal democratic state.

Brooke's legacy was to open housing. That was and is integral to Black homeownership.

VINEYARD VOICES THREE, LINSEY Lee's iconic collection of interviews with historic Vineyarders, opens, appropriately, with OLIVE TOMLINSON. (See the appendix for the Bowles family tree.)

Olive was an only child, but her grandparents Hezekiah and Olive Brown had fifteen children, five boys and ten girls. Olive had myriad cousins, many close friends, and sweet memories of summering in the Highlands of Oak Bluffs in the 1940s and '50s.

"My mother, Cutie—Olive Bowles—was a wonderful artist. She had a lot of success in a quiet kind of way. She often sold her work from our house." The proud daughter shared recollections with Linsey Lee in a 2012 interview: "She was named 'a Vineyard Treasure' by the All-Island Art Show because she kept winning."

Three of Cutie Bowles's paintings hang in Olive's living room. They are treasures. Debbie Dixon inherited several of Cutie's paintings, as her grandmother Liz White had been close with Cutie.

Olive has one painting by Lois Mailou Jones that hangs in a position of prominence. Cutie bought the piece and paid a lot for it. When Cutie gave it to Olive, Lois was annoyed because she felt no one would see it. She wanted her work in a place of prominence.

With Shearer Cottage just steps from her house, Cutie was well acquainted with the Shearers. She was close friends with Shearer cousins Miriam Walker and Liz White "So it was like a triad," recalled Olive.

Liz White was the director and motivator of the Shearer Summer Theatre. She enlisted family and friends in nearly a dozen theatrical

Olive Tomlinson's compound includes her son's house, her parents' house, and hers. Her father photographed scenes at Shearer Summer Theatre; her mother sewed actors' costumes. *Courtesy of Joyce Dresser.*

productions in the late 1940s and '50s. "The productions here on the Vineyard were magnificent," Olive recalled.

"They were at Twin Cottage: a double house, built by the ubiquitous sea captain for his two daughters, connected in the middle by a wrap-around porch. On the second level was another porch, a smaller porch. And the best part, the top, was a tower." With the audience facing the cottage, actors would enter from the woods, an open window, the balcony or even the tower. "It was just super."[125]

Of Liz White, daughter of Lily Shearer, Olive recalled, "Oh, she was wonderful. My generation marveled at how innovative and daring and charismatic they (the actors) all were. They were very dramatic, and very glamorous. They were all beauties, that's the other thing. And they would try anything."[126]

When she focused on *Othello*, "Like most of Liz's productions, it was a family affair. Liz's son, Richard Dixon, plays Iago. His wife Audrey Dixon was Desdemona." Olive added, "My father was the photographer and set builder. My Mom played Amelia. And, of course, directed by Liz White."

Cutie Bowles worked at Shearer Cottage, deftly run by Sadie Shearer. "I remember Mom was the best waitress in the world. Then one summer Gail Jackson and I, we waitressed. It took two of us to make one of her."

Olive relished the freedom and support of the Highlands community in that postwar era. The Bowles were associated with the Shearer Cottage dynasty of fun-loving, hardworking Blacks, transplanted to Martha's Vineyard each summer

Olive grew up in New York City, where she taught school and married Joe Tomlinson, one of the first Black stockbrokers. The young couple summered in The Highlands, where their two sons, John and Peter, enjoyed the ambiance and familial support of The Highlands. John and his wife have a son, Qinghua Li. Quickly they're at four generations.

Olive blossomed as a skillful tennis player and talented artist in her own right. As a denizen of The Highlands, she shares memories and stories of her youth.

Olive lives in a house built in 1910, which she had renovated in the 1970s. Her contractor, William Crabtree, upgraded it. Olive's compound includes her house, her parents' home on Church Avenue and her son Peter's house, all within sight of one another. And it is right on the Baptist Temple circle.

11

BLACK BUSINESS

In the early years of the twentieth century, Shearer Cottage served as the primary source of employment in The Highlands. Chambermaids and waitresses kept the Cottage running. Yet Shearer wasn't the only show in town. Martha Maxwell's bed-and-breakfast was also in The Highlands, a block from Myrtle Avenue.

"Mrs. Georgia O'Brien and Ms. Louisa Izett began to operate an inn for people of color."[127] Aunt Georgia's House was a guest house on lower Circuit Avenue that catered to Blacks and laborers who needed inexpensive lodging. Aunt Georgia's was listed in the *Green Book*. And it was awarded a plaque by the African American Trail of Martha's Vineyard. It has since been renamed The Tivoli.

Small cafés offered meals in The Highlands. John Pollard, a Civil War veteran, served food to vacationing Blacks. And Elizabeth Lewis managed a small dining establishment in The Highlands. Call's Market by Oak Bluffs Harbor needed bakers; Phoebe Ballou was a well-known baker at the turn of the century.

Laundresses serviced the white summer crowd. Henrietta Shearer excelled with her delivery service at the Cottage. Sarah Wentworth was also a laundress; her house was across from Harriet Peck on Dukes County Avenue. "Sarah kept a neat, plain, gray-shingled, two-story house, perhaps one of those that had been moved from the campground. It was on the edge of the wetlands in back of Sunset Lake." Mrs. Wentworth carried laundry on her bicycle, as "she pedalled [*sic*] very deliberately towards The Highlands. It was, folks recall, a sight to behold and one that commanded respect."[128]

Blacks who worked in white-run local markets or restaurants were hidden from view. Managers did not want patrons to see Blacks. This backdoor prejudice was recounted by Dean Denniston and experienced by Jocelyn Coleman Walton when she washed dishes at LaBelle's on Circuit Avenue. Oak Bluffs was segregated as were most other towns in that era.

Black men also worked in service jobs on Island, cutting hair, driving cars and positions such as painting or carpentry. David Robinson in the Campground was a caulker.

"The African American Heritage Trail of Martha's Vineyard had heard for many years about the life of Amber Wormley, and we knew that he was a business owner and local politician," wrote Elaine Weintraub in the *Martha's Vineyard Times* on February 7, 2024. World War I veteran Amber Wormley (1886–1957) bought a service station on New York Avenue in 1928. He was met by a growing demand not just for gasoline but also automobile repairs. Wormley ran his garage nearly twenty years, until he sold it to Nelson deBettencourt in 1946. The garage, deBettencourt's, is still in operation today. Wormley also handled veterans' affairs on the Vineyard. Wormley's garage will be listed on the African American Heritage Trail of Martha's Vineyard.

Robert Graves opened a machine shop on Uncas Avenue in Oak Bluffs. Graves Machine and Tool Company was recently added to the African American Heritage Trail, the trail's thirty-seventh site on Island. The business rebuilt the ring chute for the Flying Horses carousel in Oak Bluffs, built the Campground entrance arch and serviced contracts with companies like Raytheon, Polaroid, and Duracell. The business was open for 27 years. The shop's slogan was "We can repair anything except a broken heart or the crack of dawn."[129] Shirley Graves, Robert's wife, served as treasurer of the local NAACP chapter for years.

Barber Hammond cut hair in Vineyard Haven for forty years. His storefront barbershop was on Main Street, right in the line of the fire of 1883, which burned most of downtown. However, Barber Hammond successfully rebuilt his business. Martin Becker was a barber on Circuit Avenue in the summer and worked in New Bedford in the off-season. George Frye and his wife, Ella, ran a cobbler shop, also on Circuit Avenue.

A Shearer granddaughter, Liz White, was the principal of the Shearer Summer Theatre. The plays she produced from the 1940s into the 1950s were labors of love and very well appreciated. Using Twin Cottage as a stage

Amber Wormley operated this gas station in Oak Bluffs. He sold it in 1946 to Nelson deBettencourt. Today, Mike deBettencourt runs the popular service station. *Courtesy of Mike deBettencourt.*

and casting locals in the shows created a dramatic operation. Everyone in The Highlands who saw the plays enjoyed them.

Luella Coleman worked as a domestic and saved her earnings to put a down payment on Coleman Corners. And when Dorothy West finished her weekly column for the *Gazette*, she worked at the Harborside Restaurant in Edgartown.

TODAY, IT'S NOT JUST Blacks who work various jobs across the Vineyard. Black-owned businesses have proliferated on Island in the twenty-first century.

Roger Schilling has operated C'est la Vie on Circuit Avenue for thirty years. It is an enduring gift and apparel shop, a haven for Black shoppers. Roger is affable and accessible, which helps his business thrive.

India Rose is proprietor of the MV Streetwear Company on Main Street Vineyard Haven. She is motivated to make the most of her business and to help other Black-owned businesses.

Her *Martha's Vineyard Black-owned Business Directory* is in its fifth year, filled with participants.[130]

Black-run businesses are no longer an anomaly on the Vineyard. Entrepreneurs grasp the potential of a competitive environment in a tourist community.

Winston and Lisa Christie run Winston's, a takeout food shop on Oak Bluffs Harbor. In 2023, they assumed management of the popular Linda Jean's on Circuit Avenue. Black women own Biscuits, a breakfast go-to, right downtown. All summer long a line curls out the door. Eleven Circuit, owned by Chef Ralston and Mavis Francis, serves southern and Jamaican fare. The couple also run the Edgartown Diner. Chef Deon specializes in Caribbean cooking at the VFW in Oak Bluffs. And Fat Ronnie's is *the* place to go for a burger in Oak Bluffs.

Martha's Vineyard is a tourist mecca. Tourist-focused shops operate from May through October, which is a limited timeframe to market enough merchandise to generate a year-round income. "August is such a mix of crazy activity for everyone," said India Rose.

It can be challenging to be Black among white businesses competing for the same dollar. "It's easier to survive the busiest time of the season when we're recognized and accepted," noted India. The Oak Bluffs Business Association and Chamber of Commerce offer support.

Black businesspeople assess the Vineyard tourist. What are their expectations? What are they looking for? Is it a restaurant or bakery? Fine apparel or casual tees? Knick-knacks or tchotchke? People have preconceived notions. Martha's Vineyard is a vacation destination that invites curious tourists. Shopkeepers must be prepared to respond to each customer's request.

Black-owned art galleries include Zita Cousens on Circuit Avenue and Knowhere Gallery, with one location in the Arts District on Dukes County Avenue and another on Circuit Avenue. Promoting Black artists is an admirable and successful goal for these galleries.

As Black-owned businesses became integral to the Island economy, *The Martha's Vineyard Black-Owned Business Directory* offers a menu of businesses, owned and operated by Blacks, including galleries and guest houses, salons and shops. Oak Bluffs is the center, with Vineyard Haven and Edgartown part of the mix.

Kahina Van Dyke operates a trio of guest houses: Narraganset House, Dunmere-by-the-Sea, and Inkwell Beach House. She also opened a retail store, Jubilee, on Circuit Avenue, selling Vineyard vintage clothing, pictures, and memorabilia.

Valerie Moseley runs the Black and White House.

Locals take it all in, the tourists, the shopkeepers, the crowds. The Vineyard is a mix of those who live and work on Island and the visiting tourist and summer vacationers. Black businesspeople must navigate the environment, just like everyone else, doing their best to do a great job.

Marketing firms like Hoverfly (Kharma Finley-Wallace) and Shored Up Digital (Marnely Murray and Angie Prout) provide a digital presence in the Black business world. Black realtors Shelley Christiansen of Donnelly & Company and Jennifer DaSilva of Point B/Compass are standing by, promoting the next legacy property.

Black businesses are integral to the Vineyard environment. It is challenging, but eager businessmen and women are able and willing to make a success of their enterprise.

———— ⬥ ————

JOHN AND BERNICE GOLDSBERRY of Worcester learned that a house in The Highlands was about to go up for auction. Without ever seeing the house, they bought it for $2,500. It's been in the family since 1952. (See the appendix for the Goldsberry family tree.)

The house is a sprawling seven-bedroom structure abutting the Baptist Temple grounds, Rose Avenue, Dorothy West Avenue and Laurel Avenue as it morphs into Church Street. With three porches, one glassed, one screened and one open, the house is a prominent landmark in The Highlands. And if there's any question whose house it is, the nameplate on the front door reads J.J. Goldsberry, MD.

The glassed-in porch features windows from an old hotel on Circuit Avenue. The primary living room was rolled up from the Campground, decades ago, likely part of a relocated cottage. The nameboard of the whale ship *Southern Cross* nestles in the barn ceiling as the house expands further. The house has the ambiance of a sea captain's house. And it is in spotless condition, with obvious care and maintenance and décor.

Bernice, known as Babe, was Baba to her grandchildren. Babe was one of the first presidents of the Cottagers, recognized by Dorothy West in her *Vineyard Gazette* column from 1957. John was Jay or Daddy J to his grandchildren. He was a prominent Worcester physician.

The second generation of Goldsberrys followed the physician tradition. John J. Jr. and Dorista met as medical students at Howard University. As Dorista likes to say, "I graduated on Friday and got married on Saturday." John J. Jr. is a physiatrist who worked at Worcester City Hospital for decades. Dorista is a psychiatrist and former executive director of the Worcester Youth Guidance Center. At this writing, the couple are in their early nineties, living in their own home in Worcester, a home they've enjoyed for sixty years.

The nameplate on the door refers to Dr. Goldsberry, who bought this house, sight unseen, in 1952. Today, it is treasured by subsequent generations. *Photo by Thomas Dresser.*

James Goldsberry and his sister Carol are two of four siblings who share their summer home in The Highlands. Members of the fourth generation enjoy the house as well. *Courtesy of Joyce Dresser.*

John and Dorista have four children, born just past mid-century: John (1959), Yvonne (1960), James (1964) and Carol (1965). The grandparents deeded The Highlands house to their four grandchildren in 1987. James said, "They left us the house in unbelievably good shape. The gardens were great. It was a showcase." The young Goldsberrys were still in college, so they've experienced the pleasures and pitfalls, the memories, and the maintenance for most of their lives. And with a rising generation of six cousins, the house is prepped as a legacy vacation home for decades to come.

John's daughter Whitney has a three-year-old daughter herself, Amelia, who constitutes the fifth generation at the Goldsberry house.

The four siblings manage the house with a Google calendar and a commitment to keep their home in tip-top condition. The rooms are freshly painted, the bedrooms redone, and new amenities installed. The next generation, the six cousins-in-waiting, savor their time there, as they anticipate becoming custodians of their ancestors' summer home.

Even as they look ahead, the family looks back. Two organizations are researching past generations, dating to the eighteenth century. James's great-great-grandfather William Brown was a conductor on the Underground Railroad in the 1840s. And Margaret Tulip of Lexington, a Goldsberry ancestor, sued for being enslaved and won her freedom in 1768, years before the Revolution and the abolition of slavery in Massachusetts in 1783.

The Goldsberrys epitomize a family working for the common goal of enjoying and preserving the legacy of their Highlands home.

—∞—

12

BLACK CULTURE

The Age of Brooke was defined by the founding of several social organizations and activities that were part of their programmatic orbit in the summers, almost exclusively in Oak Bluffs. The Cottagers, the Oak Bluffs Tennis Club and the Shearer Summer Theatre were among the three most prominent that were overwhelmingly supported by summer residents.

This post mid-century era on the Island was built largely on the foundations of Black institutions and an insular social and cultural scene by Black residents. Support originated with institutions like Dunbar High School, Howard University, Black fraternities and sororities, the Tuskegee Airmen, and veterans of the segregated military. In this period, segregation was legally challenged, but neither Black nor white America had made corresponding structural adjustments. Social activity was still largely segregated. Black life on the Vineyard was primarily centered in Oak Bluffs. The circulation of *Ebony* and *Jet* magazines and local Black newspapers exploded. High technology was in its infancy, and the internet was not yet a reality of daily life.

Each year culinary connoisseur Dr. Jessica Harris returns to her summer home in Oak Bluffs to savor the Vineyard and share her dietary expertise and experience. "Ms. Harris's 2007 cookbook, *The Martha's Vineyard Table*, solidified her Island fame, becoming a Bible of sorts for devout Vineyard eaters."[131]

Another prominent summer Vineyarder is author Jill Nelson, whose house is on the corner of Ocean Park, just above the Inkwell. Purchased in 1968, the rambling "cottage" played a role in Nelson's 2005 "gentle memoir," *Finding Martha's Vineyard: African-Americans at Home on an Island.* She has shared the house with her three siblings, one of whom is renowned documentary filmmaker Stanley Nelson, for more than half a century. "A big house, like a long life, can accommodate many contradictions," wrote Penelope Green for the *New York Times.*[132]

As the Vineyard became more popular, there was a transition from purely social activities to forums, panels, speakers, films, and art programs focused on social justice. These programs were a result of transformative changes on Island as well as the mainland.

Professor Henry Louis Gates and Professor Charles Ogletree, both of Harvard University, recognized there was a national audience on the Vineyard, of both Black and white people thirsty for speakers and conversations about critical issues facing the nation. The Charles Hamilton Houston Institute for Race and Justice and the W.E.B. DuBois Institute for African and African American Research established by Professors Ogletree and Gates became a presence on Island.

In the summer of 2004, they assembled a panel at the Old Whaling Church in Edgartown to consider the status of a Black America on the fiftieth anniversary of the Supreme Court ruling *Brown v. Board of Education* that desegregated schools and dismantled the doctrine of separate but equal.

While Professor Charles Ogletree was moderating the panel discussion, anticipation raced around that an unannounced guest was to join the discussion. Barack Obama, then an Illinois state senator running for the U.S. Senate, entered the church and was introduced by Skip Gates: "My candidate for President in the year 2008!" This event crystallized an indelible bond between the Vineyard, Charles Ogletree, Skip Gates, and the Obamas that grew exponentially over the ensuing years.

Gates and Ogletree continued to curate forums and public dialogue on the Vineyard. Topics ranged from *Race, Gender, Age and Religion* in the 2008 election to *Between the Lines: Race and Gender in Sports* and *Grapevine: Race and Media in the 21ˢᵗ Century.*

Now known as the Hutchins Center for African and African American Research, Gates organized forums with topics like *The Rise and Fall of Affirmative Action, Culture Wars in Black and White, America's Racial Reckoning: The Pandemics and the Election, A Single Garment of Destiny, MLK's Dream in the Age of Trump, Black Millennials: They Rock but Can They Rule?, Locked Out, Locked Up: Black Men in America, The New Face of AIDS, Our Mothers, Our Sisters, Our Daughters.*

Professor Ogletree announced he had dementia, in 2016, which curtailed his Vineyard programs. In recognition of his many contributions on and off the Island, the Union Chapel Educational and Cultural Institute Inc. (UCECI) renamed its programs the Charles Ogletree Public Forum Series. Professor Ogletree passed in the summer of 2023.

Other events and programs followed, including the Martha's Vineyard African American Film Festival, the Black Comedy Festival, events by James Hester and Finding Your Roots produced by WETA, but sponsored and curated by Professor Gates. One of his most intriguing evenings included dissecting the genealogical history of political activist and academic Angela Davis and former secretary of homeland security Jeh Johnson.

Art Starts the Party is a series of art panels organized by the Pennsylvania Academy of Fine Arts and Chicago-based Clinee Hedspeth from Phillips Auction House. Art galleries focused on Black Art include Cousen Rose Gallery and the pair of Knowhere Galleries, all in Oak Bluffs.

These forums brought authors, academics, financiers, thought-leaders, polemics, and businesspeople of all stripes and diverging opinions. The Vineyard was transformed from initially focused on its social components to a center of dialogue, strategy, and action.

On the mainland, corporate America recognized that Black consumers have significant purchasing power. Publications like *Black Enterprise* pushed focused marketing and branding. Significantly, the concepts of diversity, equity, and inclusion (DEI) received broad acceptance in major corporations. Supplier diversity and shifts in recruitment of Black and female talent became an intentional strategy. Today, Blacks hold senior corporate positions reporting to the CEO with budgets to expand the companies' policies, especially firms that sell consumer-based products.

One of the most creative programs that capitalized on the explosive growth of corporate diversity, equity and inclusion is the Martha's Vineyard Chief Diversity Officer Summit created by Dani Monroe. This collection of over one hundred attendees, established in 2022, was held at the Martha's Vineyard Museum.

The transition from a largely social environment for the Black community, characterized as the Age of Brooke, to an ecosystem of intellectual, educational, cultural, business, and political events, characterized as the Age of Obama, has redefined the Vineyard community for both Black and white residents and visitors.

BIJAN BAYNE RECALLED HIS youth in The Highlands:

I first visited the Island as a child in the 1960s, staying in the cottage of my father's late grandmother, Mattie Jones. She had bought the house in The Highlands section of Oak Bluffs in 1943 after seeing an ad in a Boston newspaper. Our story was just one of many in the long history of Black residents and visitors. By the time my great-grandmother settled in the Highlands, it was an established Black summer community: home to Shearer Cottage—the first guest house to welcome Black visitors on the Island—and many distinguished residents, including Congressman Adam Clayton Powell, Jr., the writer Dorothy West, and Ralf Meshack Coleman, known as the dean of Boston's Black theater.

In those days, people like me would come for the whole summer, staying with our grandmothers or mothers while some of our fathers stayed in the city during the week to work. (The Friday evening boat, which was typically filled with fathers arriving for the weekend, was known as the "Daddy Boat.") With so much time on their hands, vacationers and neighbors got to know one another, and oftentimes became lifelong friends. It felt as if everyone in Oak Bluffs knew at least one member of every family. Small parties and cookouts hosted by Roxbury natives, such as my parents, were common. As were quiet evenings at home playing Sorry! or Scrabble. Unlike on the mainland, my parents never had to worry about my Island whereabouts from sunup to dark. My bike and the safety and quietness of the community afforded my freedom.[133]

This piece was published in *Martha's Vineyard Magazine*, used with permission. Bijan Bayne is the author of *Martha's Vineyard Basketball: How a Resort League Defied Notions of Race and Class.* (See the appendix for the Bayne family tree.)

13

BLACK POLITICS

The presence of national political figures on Martha's Vineyard began in 1874 when President Ulysses S. Grant; his wife, Julia; and the presidential party visited the Camp Meeting Association. In honor of the president, a display of fireworks and illumination was organized. This is now a major part of family life on the Vineyard, Illumination Night.

Reverend Adam Clayton Powell Sr. was part of a cohort that came to Shearer Cottage in The Highlands from New York City in the 1920s. The Powell family came to fish; it was a family affair, fishing on Long Island, Florida, the Vineyard, and places in between. Young Adam Clayton Powell returned to Oak Bluffs after he married Isabel Washington (Belle) in 1933. Belle and Adam Jr. purchased their cottage in The Highlands in 1937. Powell would be elected to Congress from Harlem in 1944 in the Seventy-Ninth Congress. The cottage remains in the family today.

Locally, the Shearer family was involved in Massachusetts politics. Herbert Jackson married Doris Pope, granddaughter of Charles and Henrietta Shearer. Jackson had a long and illustrious career in politics, beginning with his election to the Massachusetts legislature in 1950. Doris's brother, Lincoln Pope, was also elected to the state legislature, serving from 1957 to 1964.

Royal Bolling Sr. from Boston and Narragansett Avenue in Oak Bluffs was elected to the Massachusetts legislature in 1961, moving to the state senate in 1982. His sons Royal Bolling Jr. and Bruce Bolling followed suit, serving in the legislature (1972) and the Boston City Council (1981), respectively. Bruce Bolling became the first Black president of the Boston City Council.

As noted earlier, Edward W. Brooke was elected attorney general of Massachusetts in 1962. Brooke went on to become the first popularly elected Black senator in the United States. And he vacationed in Oak Bluffs more than half a century.

Powell and Brooke led a bevy of Washington politicians to the sun, fun and frivolity of the Vineyard over the years.

From the 1950s into the 1970s, the red-roofed Villa Rosa on Sea View Avenue near the Inkwell was known as the Summer White House. Prominent Black politicians, leaders, and stars vacationed at this private home, courtesy of labor leader Joseph Overton. Guests included A. Phillip Randolph, Harry Belafonte, Ralph Abernathy, Sammy Davis Jr., and Martin Luther King.

Established by owner Joe Overton in the mid-1950s, Villa Rosa was the twentieth-century Summer White House for the civil rights movement. Guests included Coretta and Martin Luther King Jr., Malcolm X, CB Powell, Mel Patrick, Bayard Rustin, Jesse Jackson, and Harry Belafonte among others. *Photo by Thomas Dresser.*

EDUCATION IS A STEP removed from politics and key to the success of any community. Martha's Vineyard has been fortunate to employ energetic, quality educators in Island schools. From Rufus Shorter to Kriner Cash, the role of superintendent has been a key leadership position. Bob Tankard led West Tisbury School as principal for many years. And several highly qualified Black teachers served in the school system: Quentin Bannister, Wanza and Bettie Davis, Janice and Leo Frame, Helen Manning, and Carmen Wilson.

As elected officials continued to come to the Island, an iconic photo for many Blacks symbolized why summering on the Vineyard could be a welcoming experience. It was a photo of President Bill Clinton and his friend Vernon Jordan, civil rights icon. The photo captured them riding in a golf cart on the Farm Neck Golf Course in Oak Bluffs. The intriguing part was that President Clinton was driving, not Jordan. This 1994 photo was talked about for its symbolism. What it said to many was that perhaps on Martha's Vineyard race and status mean less than friendship. Maybe this is a place with its history and demographic mix of local islanders, Portuguese, Native Americans, Cape Verdeans, Jamaicans, and Brazilians, where we can find peace and harmony.

Valerie Jarrett visited the Vineyard for many years. She invited Barack and Michelle Obama and their family to the Vineyard after Barack's electrifying speech at the Democratic National Convention in Boston in the summer of 2004. The visit ignited a love affair with the Vineyard. And following his presidency, the Obamas purchased a home on the Vineyard: a seven-bedroom 6,892-square-foot beach house set on almost thirty acres of land by Edgartown Great Pond.

The Obama halo added significantly to the Black summer and full-time residents and tourists on Martha's Vineyard.

IN THE 2000S, A Victorian house on Temahigan in Oak Bluffs became the political and philanthropic focal point for Black politicians. Judy and Ron Davenport graciously opened their doors to candidates and supporters in multiple elections, beginning with Barack Obama in 2007. As Richard Taylor noted, the Davenports have "become de facto leaders of a small circle of black Vineyard residents who truly understand the social, cultural, political, and civic value of leveraging the Vineyard people and place for the larger diaspora."[134]

Ron and Judy Davenport made their Victorian Newport-style cottage available as the venue for Barack Obama's first fundraiser on the Vineyard. Picking up from Joe Overton at Villa Rose, the Davenport cottage became the twenty-first-century Summer White House for the civil rights movement. *Photo by Thomas Dresser.*

The *Boston Globe* sought to evaluate the political power of Blacks on Island today. "Modern luminaries like the Obamas and Spike Lee own homes on the island. With the increase in events geared toward a Black audience in August, the island is only getting more popular."

"Don't underestimate the Barack-ism," joked Steve Capers.[135]

Politicians and donors find a welcoming atmosphere on the Vineyard for their campaigns. National leaders address fundraisers and forums in prominent public speaking opportunities.

"It's like gumbo—everybody's mixing things in and, you know, you're creating this recipe for excellence," said Capers, who, with his wife, owns the Strand Theatre in Oak Bluffs and puts on an annual comedy show on Island featuring Black comics. They also host fundraisers there for Black politicians.

Philip J. Allston (1860–1915) was the first Allston to visit Martha's Vineyard; he vacationed on Island with his family at the turn of the century, around 1900.

Philip J. Allston attended the New England College of Pharmacy and worked as a manufacturing druggist at Potter Drug and Chemical Corporation. He enhanced the effectiveness of Cuticura Antibacterial Medicated Soap, the company's primary product.

Allston was vice president of the National Negro Business League, under founder and president Booker T. Washington. He was a ham radio operator and involved in the formation of the Black Tennis Association.

Allston's son, Philip R. Allston, grew up in Oak Bluffs. Dorothy, his wife, met him when she summered on the Vineyard. "Philip R. Allston attended MIT, hoping to become an architect, but this field was difficult for people of color, so he entered a new career: electronics and radio. He worked on radar systems at the Boston Naval Shipyard," according to his son, Carroll.

"The Allston house, at 74 Meadow Avenue, was purchased in 1957 from Merrill Thomas, who, at that time, sold most of the houses to minorities," said Carroll, who has retired from his position as an engineer with the MBTA. The house is still in the family.

Carroll's wife is Myrna Allston. Myrna has moderated the Cottagers' annual fashion show since 1989. She served as president of the Cottagers from 1994 to 1999. For twenty-five years, Myrna modeled at the Copley Seven Modeling Agency in Boston and ran Myrna's Boutique at Coolidge Corner. And she operated a daycare program. Myrna is a retired Boston public school teacher.

Carroll and Myrna have two daughters, Malika (b. 1982) and Carolyn (b. 1988). Malika is a senior financial analyst. Carolyn married on the Vineyard in 2022; she and her husband have a son, Darius Trenteetun. They live in Minnesota, where Carolyn is a school principal; her husband, Jethro, is a corporate attorney for General Mills.

Darius Trenteetun enjoyed his first summer on the Vineyard in 2023; he represents the fifth generation of Allstons on Martha's Vineyard.

14

MISSTEPS

Since the relocation of thirty Black families from the Camp Meeting Association, skirmishes and blemishes have occurred on Island. Prejudice has been evident, from home purchasing to hotel refusals to refusal of club membership. Blacks have endured racist taunts and incidents over the years.

A few current issues deserve discussion.

"The chasm is closed," read a plaque on the soldier statue in Ocean Park. "In memory of the restored Union, this tablet is dedicated by Union veterans of the Civil War and patriotic citizens of Martha's Vineyard in honor of the Confederate soldiers." Clennon King, a summer visitor from Georgia, took umbrage with those words and advocated its removal in 2019.

People of color feel no obligation to respect Confederate soldiers. "We do not honor treason or those who fought to continue the institution of slavery," Gretchen Tucker Underwood, a leader of the Martha's Vineyard NAACP, told the board of selectmen.

The offensive plaque was removed to the Martha's Vineyard Museum.[136] Clennon King seeks additional explanation of the wording on the plaque.

JUNETEENTH BECAME A NATIONAL holiday in 2022. However, the Oak Bluffs select board refused to permit the NAACP to fly the Juneteenth flag on town land. Local NAACP president Arthur Hardy-Doubleday cited the interim flag policy. "Juneteenth has long had deep significance to African Americans and to the Oak Bluffs community, and this year for the first time it's being celebrated as both a federal and a state holiday. We believe that the town of Oak Bluffs should be observing it too," he said in a news release.[137]

⸻

JACKIE ROBINSON SERVED THREE terms as president of the Boston NAACP. As a seasonal resident since the 1950s, Robinson opened a tennis club on his New York Avenue property. He was unsuccessful in expanding his resort and eventually unable to hold onto the property. This exemplifies a downfall of legacy homeownership. Robinson passed in 2006.[138]

⸻

"POLICE ON MARTHA'S VINEYARD are asking for the public's help after signs promoting a white nationalist group appeared over the weekend around the town of Oak Bluffs, a popular summer destination for Black families."[139] The *Boston Globe* article in September 2023 was a wake-up call to Vineyarders who feel immune from hate-group rhetoric.

Four handmade signs were posted near Black-owned businesses. Wording was consistent with the white supremacist group Patriot Front. The article concluded, "A place rich with Black history, Oak Bluffs is home to Shearer Cottage, an inn that catered to African Americans when it opened in 1912, and the Inkwell, a historic beach destination for Black families."

Current NAACP president Toni Kauffman recommends not giving the racist group any oxygen, but supporting Black and Indigenous-owned businesses, actively responding to racist actions through the NAACP or BLM groups and becoming involved politically by voting.

⸻

IN LINSEY LEE'S 2015 interview with VERA SHORTER in *Vineyard Voices Three*, the origin of Vera's commitment to community, family and social activism emerges. At the age of ten or eleven, on Long Island, Vera found herself living near a migrant camp. She recalled, "I would walk over there, and I'd get about four, five or six of them and get ready to go to church on Sundays." Reaching out to those less fortunate proved a hallmark throughout her long life.

Vera Shorter (1923–2021) supervised auditors for twenty-five years with the Internal Revenue System and contributed a column to a Brooklyn newspaper, the *Community Chatter*. When Rufus and Vera Shorter moved to Martha's Vineyard, Vera epitomized life as a joiner and doer.

Vera and Rufus Shorter (1920–1980) married in 1943. "We came years back, in the '50s, for a visit with the children when they were little. We had heard about the Vineyard. We always said, 'Let's go to the Vineyard!'"[140] They fell in love with Martha's Vineyard after several visits with Island friends and purchased property in Sea Glen in 1973. When Rufus Shorter was hired as the first Black superintendent of schools in 1976, they moved to a house overlooking the Lagoon, a house still in the family. The Shorters' daughters and grandson recognize the power of property and intend to hold on to the family legacy.

Rufus Shorter was involved with the Nathan Mayhew Seminars and worked out a program for Island teachers to get master's degrees through the Seminars. Sixteen teachers earned their degrees. He was also responsible for construction of the Performing Art Center at the high school. Unfortunately, Rufus Shorter passed in 1980 at the age of sixty.

While grieving for her husband on a trip to California, Vera wanted to come home. Home, she realized, was her house on the Lagoon; that proved to be her headquarters for the next forty years as she lived a life in a whirlwind of community activism.

"I was a member of the Association for the Study of Negro Life and History when I was about 17," Vera told Linsey Lee in the 2015 interview. And she continued to join. Among other programs, Vera was a member of the Lagoon Pond Association, the Literacy Program, the Duke Ellington Society, and the NAACP. She worked tirelessly, fundraising, organizing, and communicating with Islanders. She enjoyed participation in two book groups. She was busy.

In the interview, Vera observed, "It's hard to describe the Vineyard, because on one hand it's serene and beautiful and quiet and nice. And then on the other hand it gets raucous and mean. So, it does reflect the greater outside—off-Island part of the world. It does reflect some of that, too. But basically, it is a nice place to be, you know? I think we all agree on that."[141]

The Shorters' daughters, Lynn and Beth, and grandson, Gabriel Bagot, agree on the importance of holding their home. They understand the challenge to protect a house even when one doesn't live on-site. And they recognize the challenge to purchase Vineyard property in the current market.

Beth Bagot said "For twenty years my sister Lynn and I have alternated spending about five months each year with my mother. When she died two years ago, we maintained that arrangement to keep the house."

Beth Bagot is a retired Alvin Ailey dancer and language teacher. She splits her year between Vineyard Haven and France. Her sister, Lynn Shorter, a poet and lecturer, lives in England, with time in the Vineyard house.

Beth's son, Gabriel, earned his MBA and garnered experience in real estate and hotel management. For more than a year, he co-managed Lark

Vera Shorter is surrounded by one of her daughters, Beth Bagot, and Beth's son Gabriel. Their Vineyard Haven home represents three generations of Black homeownership. *Courtesy of Beth Bagot.*

hotels in Edgartown, including The Christopher, The Edgar, The Sydney and The Richard. He worked at Summercamp in Oak Bluffs. Currently, Gabriel Bagot lives in California and works at Booking.com.

Of her mother's social activism, Beth compared it to the post-enslavement era when clubs and social gatherings brought formerly enslaved people together for support. Vera's wry comment, "The Cottagers don't need Vera Shorter," came from an interview with Linsey Lee. Beth added that her mother "also mentioned that there were many accomplished women who did good works and had a sense of humour and she did a dance routine with/for them." That was Vera, the life of the party.

Beth said, "It was always difficult for struggling Blacks to make ends meet, at the same time trying to get ahead. It's a challenge to hold onto property, especially if it is a second home, a vacation house. And when property is sold, the homeowner loses the culture of the community. That's what happened in Sag Harbor, when Blacks sold their vacation property to the highest bidder; they lost their standing in the community."

"Today we know how important it is to hold onto vacation property or any property period, that has historical value for us." That's the challenge, and the goal, of so many legacy homeowners.

15

LEGACY HOMEOWNERSHIP

I t is important to understand how Black property ownership on the Vineyard evolved. The service class—cooks, chauffeurs, maids—and early entrepreneurs comprised the first wave of Black people who bought on Island. Early places like Shearer Cottage in The Highlands served not only as a bed-and-breakfast but as a social cocoon for Black families and seasonal visitors.

We commend those people who shared their stories about preserving their Black-owned homes. As homeowners know too well, maintaining an old house is a reminder of the income required for seasonal homeownership. An escrow account funds capital expenses and upkeep. Also, a line of succession, as spelled out by Sadie Shearer, holds on to a family property.

In the mid-twentieth century, homeownership spread from The Highlands to the School Street District by Dukes County Avenue and the Copeland District by the Inkwell and Seaview Avenue.

This led to the formation of Black organizations and institutions that created a sense of community to the Vineyard in general and Oak Bluffs in particular. Shearer Summer Theater, the Cottagers and the Oak Bluffs Tennis Club gave summer residents platforms for structured events for themselves and their families. That sense of racial comfort proved a worthy option for W.E.B. Du Bois's "double consciousness." Oak Bluffs offers an accepting, comfortable environment.[142]

Over time Black homeownership spread throughout the Island, including Vineyard Haven, Edgartown, East Chop, Chilmark, Chappaquiddick, West

Tisbury, and Aquinnah. This rise in Black homeownership was financed in part by young professionals with successful jobs and stock options that significantly increase Black wealth, thus magnifying the opportunity to purchase more expensive homes.

More professionals entered private equity and venture capital firms. With the business focus on diversity, equity, and inclusion, this led to a new cadre of Black executives. Corporate and fund boards made seats for more diverse members. In 2022, Kahina Van Dyke hosted a luncheon for Black women who served on corporate boards. Oak Bluffs' own Dani Monroe founded a chief diversity officer conference on the Vineyard. National corporations recognize Blacks wield significant consumer power.

Additionally, programs, forums, live entertainment, and film festivals proliferate, creating the sense of community. Morehouse College and Howard University welcome students and alumni to the Vineyard for programs and reunions. James Hester productions, Steven Anglin, Colin Redd, House on the Vineyard, Camp Meeting programs, Inkwell Beach outings, Jack and Jill, Hutchins Forums, Juneteenth Jubilee and Union Chapel Educational and Cultural Institute combine to make the Island comfortable for all.

Reminders of the past, on Island and the mainland, are warning signs along the roadway of Black homeownership. We acknowledge setbacks in Black homeownership caused by eminent domain. However, it is unlikely The Highlands need fear another Seneca Village swallowed up by Central Park; Ocean Park is the town park. Another Manhattan Beach or East Chop Beach Club is unlikely; the Inkwell is a town beach, open to all.

The Vineyard is not perfect. We have our newspaper diatribes, town meeting angry voices, protests at Five Corners. Yet we are safe. Keys are left in the car, houses unlocked, flower and farm stands untended. The Vineyard projects an aura of access, tranquility, safety, and respect.

Nationally, the 1921 Tulsa riot was hidden from history. We must face our collective past. And we have issues in our backyard. A coda to the research of Andrew Patch is in order. He uncovered the mystery and history of the relocated Campground cottages and the practice that excluded Blacks from owning Campground cottages for nearly a century. Those decisions shame us all. Nothing was redemptive in the Methodists' measures.

Still, it is our responsibility to recognize such action was not uncommon at the time: see Central Park in the 1850s and Manhattan Beach in the 1920s. As Jane Melcney Coe wrote, "I really appreciate what you are doing in more ways than one. What I got from it is that you are taking information which leaves everyone feeling outraged and sad and following up with more context and what came next. Being kicked out of the camp grounds is not the end of the story at all. Hooray! Recognize, accept, even honor the hurt and harm but move on from there. I like it. I really like it."

The loss of homeownership as has occurred in Sag Harbor is highly unlikely, given the more than one thousand Black-owned cottages all over the Vineyard. At Sag Harbor, Black-owned property has been bought by developers from the Hamptons who tear down the legacy property, build their development, and make a hefty profit. Yes, the Black homeowner gets some money, but the community loses its historic Black patina. (And we know money in the pocket is harder to hold than a family manse.)

The presence of Black real estate brokers like Jennifer DaSilva, Shelley Christenson, Sandra Graham, Amy Goldson, and others ensure access to land and cottages for new owners and keep legacy properties in the family when there are sales. Jennifer DaSilva offered this observation on her success as an Island realtor: "I sell homes to homebuyers of all races, colors and creeds in all of the 6 towns on our island. Edgartown is very popular. Of the 20+ homes that I sold this year (2023), to clients who identify as Black or African American, only about 50% were in Oak Bluffs. Fortunately, people can choose to live wherever they want now!"[143]

Increasingly, Black retirees live year-round on the Vineyard, extending the presence of Black residents in all phases of Vineyard life.

Black Americans have always sought to find peace, physical and psychological comfort, recognizing we are constantly trying to live in a world of "double consciousness," which is, according to W.E.B. Du Bois, "for a man to be both a Negro and an American." For generations, the Vineyard has stood for racial comfort if only for just a few short summer months. It offers a balm to those who come for a day, a weekend, a month, or a season, only to return to the mainland to face more institutionalized challenges of living in a nation still striving to be a more perfect Union.

The foundation initially built by the vision and values of Black Americans coupled with a small but distinct middle class that held on to the Island with an unrelenting grasp, while providing a nexus to the next generation, has catapulted the bounce of their children, grandchildren, and their progeny for generations to come.

EPILOGUE

We asked Shelley Christiansen, an Island realtor, to share her thoughts on Black legacy properties.

Paulette [not her real name] *traveled to Oak Bluffs from North Carolina on a mission. She had her posse in tow— two adult daughters, a brother, and a sister-in-law. She was set on finally scoring a family vacation home.*

Paulette fondly remembered many a childhood summer in the fifties and sixties at her grandmother's former home, a vintage cottage with farmhouse porch within flip-flopping distance of Circuit Avenue and the beach. Paulette has now rebooted the legacy with a similar cottage for her own grandchildren and for the generations to come.

As real estate brokers—anywhere in the world—we become acquainted with family legacy homes at one of two stages: When the legacies begin or when they end. When the dawn of a legacy home is intentional, it's joyful and promising. The endings are sentimental, at best.

Here on the Vineyard, legacies end for a variety of reasons: A required sale for the settlement of an estate. A court order to settle a tax lien. The unmanageable expense of restoring a withering antique. The desire of, say, six siblings or fourteen grandchildren to go their separate ways—to a newer subdivision with easy-care homes on the outskirts of town, or as far as California. Inevitably, at least one family member is unhappy with the demise. Hard grudges endure.

Meantime, the next owners of the home come to know—and even appreciate—that "their" house will forever be known to the neighbors as Mrs. So-and-So's house. Mrs. So-and-So's grease canister may still be on a kitchen shelf.

Between the dawning and the sunset, many a legacy home stays alive for the very long haul. As a realtor, I look into the eyes of certain young grandchildren and great-grandchildren and know: This one will never let the family home go. When her time comes as matriarch, she'll have the passion as well as the means to keep the legacy alive.

―◆◆◆―

APPENDIX

The following family trees were provided by Jane Meleney Coe in her *Guide to East Chop Families*.

———✦———

WE ENCOURAGE A VISIT to these national museums on Black history in the United States:

Memphis National Civil Rights Museum at the Lorraine Motel in Memphis, Tennessee | civilrightsmuseum.org
National Museum of African American History and Culture in Washington, D.C. | nmaahc.si.edu

———✦———

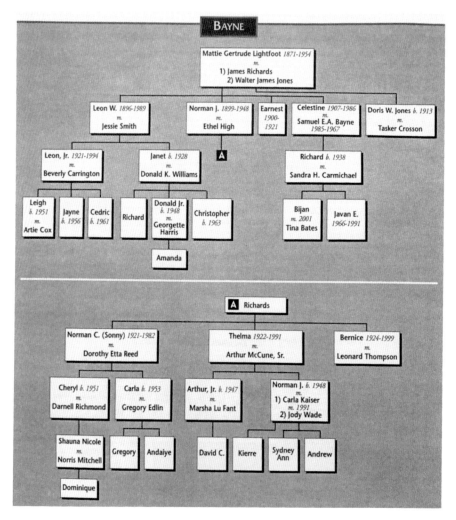

The Bayne family house on Myrtle Avenue sits among the houses of the Powells, the Wests and Coleman Corners, all Black legacy homes. *Courtesy of Jane Meleney Coe.*

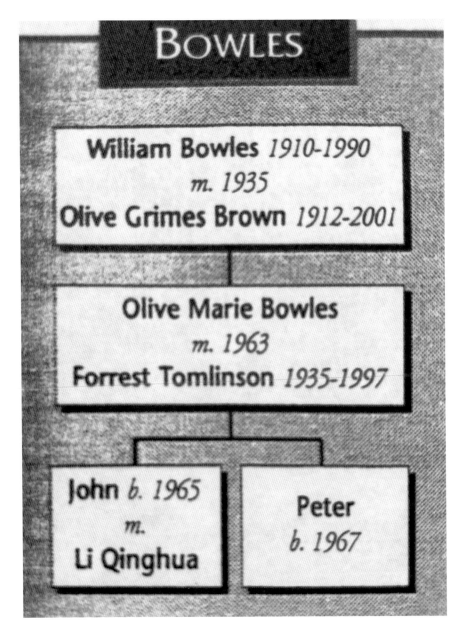

BOWLES

William Bowles *1910-1990*
m. 1935
Olive Grimes Brown *1912-2001*

Olive Marie Bowles
m. 1963
Forrest Tomlinson *1935-1997*

John *b. 1965*
m.
Li Qinghua

Peter
b. 1967

Olive Tomlinson has one grandson, Li Qinghua, born in 2012. *Courtesy of Jane Meleney Coe.*

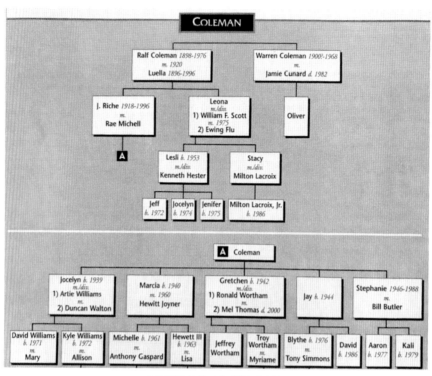

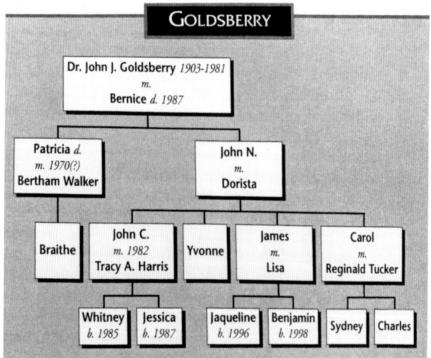

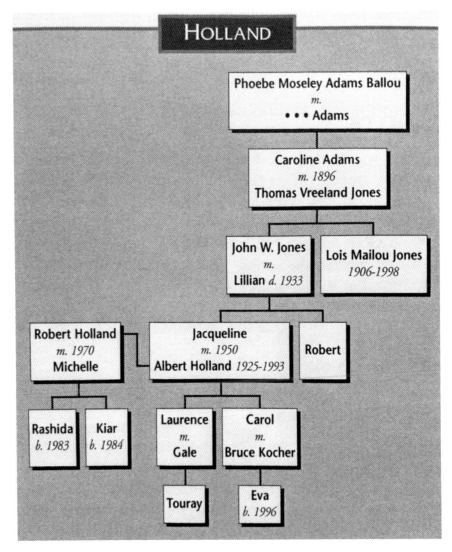

HOLLAND

Phoebe Moseley Adams Ballou
m.
• • • **Adams**

Caroline Adams
m. 1896
Thomas Vreeland Jones

John W. Jones
m.
Lillian *d. 1933*

Lois Mailou Jones
1906-1998

Robert Holland
m. 1970
Michelle

Jacqueline
m. 1950
Albert Holland *1925-1993*

Robert

Rashida
b. 1983

Kiar
b. 1984

Laurence
m.
Gale

Carol
m.
Bruce Kocher

Touray

Eva
b. 1996

Above: Lois Mailou Jones had no children. *Courtesy of Jane Meleney Coe.*

Opposite, top: The following updates refer to the Coleman family tree. Ralf Meshack Coleman married Luella Barnett. J. Richie and Rae Wiggins divorced. Leona Coleman (1924–2018) and William Scott divorced. Marcia Coleman was born in 1940. Ronald Wortham died in 2023. Jay "Bo" Coleman died in 2022. Duncan Walton died in 2022. David Williams died in 2022. *Courtesy of Jane Meleney Coe.*

Opposite, bottom: Of the current generation in the Goldsberry house, Yvonne married Cherie Harris. Carol is divorced. Her children are Sydney (1994) and Charles (1996). John C's daughter Whiney is married to Charles Smith. Their daughter, Amelia Smith, born in 2019, represents the fifth generation of Goldsberrys in The Highlands house. *Courtesy of Jane Meleney Coe.*

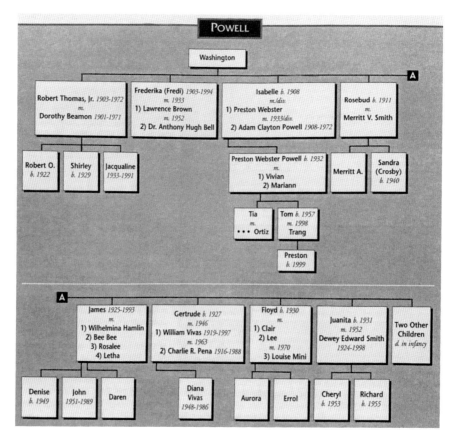

The Powell family still visits Bunny Cottage on the corner of Dorothy West Avenue and Myrtle Avenue in The Highlands. The plaque by their house celebrates the story of Adam Clayton Powell Jr. and Isabel. *Courtesy of Jane Meleney Coe.*

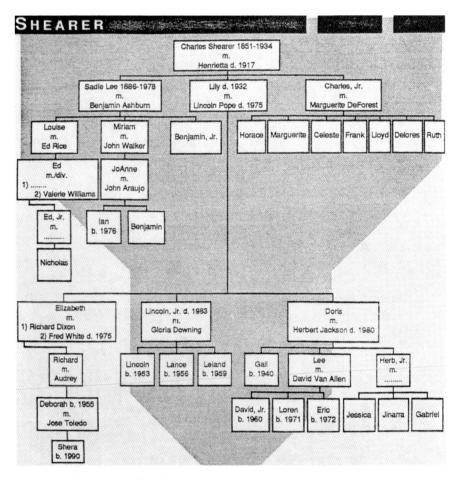

Of Shearer Cottage, Lee Van Allen updated her children's information.

David Jr., born in 1964, married Angela Rue and had three children: Camille, Kendall, and Kennedi.

Loren was born in 1968, never married, and had no children.

Eric, born in 1971, married Carma Burnette and had two children: Oren and Jared.

Descendants of Charles Shearer Jr. and his wife, Marguerite, lived in Boston.

Debbie Dixon passed in July 2023. *Courtesy of Jane Meleney Coe.*

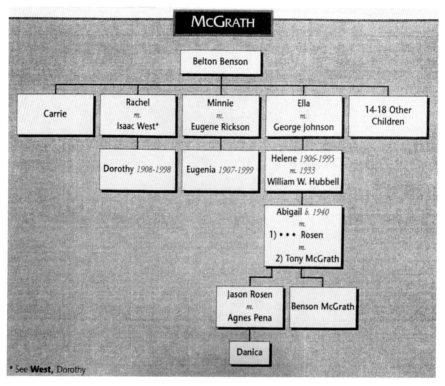

Benjamin Belton Benson (b. 1850) and Helen Benson (b. 1853).
Of eighteen siblings, Rachel Benson married Isaac West, daughter Dorothy (1907–1998).
Abigail McGrath (b. 1940) married Leonard Rosen, and later, Tony McGrath
Son: Jason Rosen (b. 1961) married Agnes Pena; their daughter is Danica.
Son: Benson McGrath (b. 1971) *Courtesy of Jane Meleney Coe.*

NOTES

1. Landownership

1. Library of Congress, "The Founder and the Vote," https://www.loc.gov/classroom-materials/elections/right-to-vote/the-founders-and-the-vote/.
2. Skip Finley, "A Bell of Freedom," *Martha's Vineyard*, https://mvmagazine.com/news/2021/07/08/bell-freedom.
3. Ibid.
4. Ibid.

2. Owning Property

5. George Henry Moore, *Notes on the History of Slavery in Massachusetts*, via Internet Archive, https://archive.org/details/notesonhistorys01moorgoog/page/n150/mode/2up.
6. Kerri Lee Alexander, "Elizabeth Freeman (1744? –1829)," National Women's History Museum, https://www.womenshistory.org/education-resources/biographies/elizabeth-freeman.
7. Ibid.
8. *Never Caught*, by Erica Dunbar, documents the life of Oney Judge Staines (1773–1848), enslaved to Martha Washington. Oney escaped in 1796. The president made every effort to recapture her. She lived half a century as a free woman in Greenland, New Hampshire.

9. The steam locomotive arrived in the 1840s. Thousands of enslaved people (freight) made their way north, following the network (schedule) of safe houses (stations), from one abolitionist (conductor) to another, along a secure route (line) to freedom. Assisting runaway enslaved people was illegal. Whites who aided runaways were subject to arrest, fines of $1,000, and sentences of six months' incarceration.

10. Scott Shane, "How the Underground Got Its Name," *New York Times*, September 9, 2023, https://www.nytimes.com/2023/09/11/opinion/man-who-named-underground-railroad.html

11. Jacqueline Holland, "The African American Presence on Martha's Vineyard," *Dukes County Intelligencer*, now the *MV Quarterly*, August 1991.

12. Ibid.

13. Ibid.

14. Ibid.

3. The Highlands

15. *Vineyard Gazette*, August 23, 1878.

16. Recollections by Abby McGrath.

17. Dorothy West, afterword to *The Living Is Easy* (Old Westbury, NY: Feminist Press, 1982), 362.

18. Dorothy West, *The Wedding* (New York: Doubleday Publishing, 1995), 2.

4. Blacks Excluded

19. Lloyd Hare, *Martha's Vineyard: A Short History and Guide* (Edgartown, MA: Dukes County Historical Society, 1956).

20. Edited by Eleanor Ransom Mayhew, 27.

21. Bilal G. Morris, "There's a Black Village Under Central Park That Was Founded by Alexander Hamilton's Secret Black Son," Newsone, November 1, 2021, https://newsone.com/4242055/was-sencea-village-founded-by-alexander-hamiltons-secret-black-son/

22. Central Park Conservancy, https://www.centralparknyc.org.

23. Seneca Village consisted of about fifty houses with a population of 225 Blacks. It boasted three churches, two cemeteries and an African American school. "The settlement was a rare haven of Black homeownership," wrote Greg Melville in his history of Seneca Village, *Over My Dead Body*. The media described Seneca Village as a settlement of shanties, with vagrants and homeless scoundrels. Seneca Village was absorbed into Central Park through

eminent domain. Work commenced in 1858. "According to one newspaper, 'the supremacy of the law was upheld by the policeman's bludgeons.'"

24. Following the 2020 death of George Floyd, a nationwide outpouring of support grew for justice to the Black community. Los Angeles County supervisor Janice Hahn said, "This fight has always been about what is best for the Bruce family, and they feel what is best for them is selling this property back to the County for nearly $20 million and finally rebuilding the generational wealth they were denied for nearly a century." She added, "This is what reparations look like and it is a model that I hope governments across the country will follow."

25. "LA County Supervisors Vote to Return Bruce's Beach to Owners' Descendants," CBS News, April 20, 2021, https://www.cbsnews.com/losangeles/news/la-county-votes-to-return-bruces-beach-to-owners-descendants/.

26. Andrew Patch, "First Cottagers of Color," *MV Quarterly*, August 2021, 7.

27. Edward Oakes, "John Wesley: A Biography," *First Things*, December 2004, https://www.firstthings.com/article/2004/12/john-wesley-a-biography.

28. "John and Charles Wesley: Reviewers of the Church (3 Mar 1791)," http://satucket.com/lectionary/Wesley.htm.

29. Thomas Dresser, *The Rise of Tourism on Martha's Vineyard* (Charleston, SC: The History Press, 2020), 107.

30. *Martha's Vineyard Herald*, July 13, 1889.

31. Patch, "First Cottagers of Color," 10.

32. *Boston Herald*, July 17, 1889.

33. Arthur Railton, "Widow Rocker, Part Indian, Struggles to Break the Chains of Poverty," *Dukes County Intelligencer*, February 2006, 79–90.

5. Black Legacy

34. Shelley Christiansen, "The Shearer Family, Keepers of the Inn," *Martha's Vineyard Magazine*, June 2012.

35. Ibid.

36. Meleney, Shearer family members: Doris Jackson, Liz White, and Lee Van Allen (Jane Meleney Coe, *A Guide to East Chop Families 2001* [self-published, 2002]).

37. Ibid.

38. Christiansen, "Shearer Family."

39. Ibid.

40. Ibid.

6. Racial Conflicts

41. Louis Menand, "The Civil Rights Showdown Nobody Remembers," *The New Yorker*, August 7, 2023.
42. Ibid.
43. Heather Cox Richardson, *Letters from an American*, February 13, 2023, https://heathercoxrichardson.substack.com, .
44. Ibid.
45. Ibid.
46. Nicole Chavez, "Tulsa Massacre Survivor at 107 Years Old Testifies That the Horror of That Day Never Goes Away," CNN, May 20, 2021, www.cnn.com/2021/05/19/us/tulsa-massacre-survivors-congress/index.html.
47. Ibid.
48. Wesley Lowery, "Viola Fletcher Waited 102 Years for Reparations. She's Still Waiting," *Washington Post*, October 4, 2023, https://www.washingtonpost.com/style/power/2023/10/04/tulsa-massacre-viola-fletcher-reparations/.
49. Three groups asked Hubert to go to the Vineyard: The Society for the Propagation of the Gospel Among the Indians and Others of North America, the Massachusetts Baptist Missionary Society, and the Massachusetts Board of Education
50. Thomas Dresser, *African Americans of Martha's Vineyard* (Charleston, SC: The History Press, 2010), 67.
51. Phyllis Meras, "Aquinnah's Huberts," *Martha's Vineyard Magazine*, 2013.
52. Ibid.
53. Margaret Sanger papers, https://documents.alexanderstreet.com/d/1000688024.
54. Ibid.

7. Court Cases

55. Linsey Lee, *More Vineyard Voices: Words, Faces and Voices of Island People* (Edgartown, MA: Martha's Vineyard Museum, 2019), 148
56. Jocelyn Walton, *The Place My Heart Calls Home: Stories of a Working Class African-American Family from Boston to Martha's Vineyard* (Weymouth, MA: A Nickel Down Publishing, 2018), 131.
57. Richardson, *Letters from an American*, June 1, 2023.

58. Will Kenton, "Zoning Ordinance: Definition, Types of Regulations, Pros and Cons," Investopedia, March 9, 2022, https://www.investopedia.com/terms/z/zoning-ordinance.asp.

59. Richard Taylor, *Race, Property, and the Power of Place* (Cambridge, MA: Harvard Book Store, 2016), 323.

60. *Buchanan v. Warley* (1917) overturned zoning regulations to separate housing by race. Legally restrictive racial zoning was forbidden. "The *Buchanan v. Warley* decision began to level the playing field somewhat in the fight against housing discrimination on America's mainland," wrote Richard Taylor in *Race, Property, and the Power of Place*. The court refused to require separate blocks of housing for Blacks and whites, as *Plessey* suggested. "This decision sounded the death knell for legally separating neighborhoods in America."

61. Taylor, *Race, Property, and the Power*, 328.

62. "What has been missing from the analyses of Brown and Shelley over the years is the relationship between the two cases. Employment and income data suggest a very high correlation between the quality of one's education and one's income and earning capacity. A strong argument can be made that the Shelley case, and all that followed, in fact established that housing options can deliver broader access to full citizen options. The location of one's house determines retail services, multiple services, and access to employment, school, and cultural opportunities and green spaces" (Taylor, *Race, Property, and the Power*, 332).

63. Taylor, *Race, Property, and the Power*, 325.

64. Ibid., 223.

65. Ibid., 225–26.

66. Ibid., 227.

67. Ibid., 226.

68. *Vineyard Gazette,* January 5, 2022.

69. *Vineyard Gazette*, March 12, 1937.

70. Email summary from Jeffrey Burnett, September 12, 2013.

71. "Research identified that the Tabernacle was supported by at least forty-seven 8 by 8-inch wooden posts. These posts were installed on cement footings, nearly all of which survive today. It was also found that the Tabernacle has a cement floor that was likely added some time after the initial construction in 1877–1878" (email from Jeffrey Burnett on September 12, 2023).

8. *The* Green Book

72. As the crowds diminished, Idlewild's businesses and resorts closed. By 2019, the population of Idlewild had sunk to fewer than one thousand, with dozens of vacant buildings. Idlewild treasures its rewarding past, where leisure activities drew Black tourists to a community on the shores of Lake Idlewild.

73. "On Long Island, A Beachfront Haven for Black Families," *New York Times Style Magazine*, October 1, 2020, https://www.nytimes.com/2020/10/01/t-magazine/sag-harbor.html

74. Ibid.

75. Jenn Barthole, "Sag Harbor's Historic Black Beachfront Community," Ebony, https://www.ebony.com/sag-harbors-historic-black-beachfront-community-highlighted-on-home-docu-series

76. Andrew Kahrl, *The Land Was Ours* (Chapel Hill: University of North Carolina Press, 2016), eBook.

77. Dresser, *African Americans of Martha's Vineyard*, 108.

78. Christiansen, "Shearer Family."

79. Taylor, *Race, Property, and the Power*, 111.

80. Ibid.

81. Lavanya Ramanathan, "How Martha's Vineyard Became a Black Summertime Sanctuary," Vox, August 24, 2021, https://www.vox.com/the-highlight/22627047/marthas-vineyard-black-tourism-oak-bluffs-inkwell

82. Taylor, *Vineyard Gazette* town column, February 24, 2023.

83. Ibid.

84. Higgins, "A Vineyard Vignette," *MV Times*, February 16, 2023.

85. Cromwell, "The History of Oak Bluffs as a Popular Resort for Blacks," *Dukes County Intelligencer*, August 1984.

86. Walton, *Place My Heart Calls Home*, 23.

87. Ibid., 108.

88. Ibid., 105.

89. Ibid., 109.

90. Ibid., 128.

91. Riche, "Being Black in Old Oak Bluffs: A Remembrance of the Joys and the Sorrows," *Vineyard Gazette*, August 20, 1971.

92. Dorothy West, *Vineyard Gazette* town column, March 27, 1992.

93. Walton, *Place My Heart Calls Home*, 65.

94. Ibid., 136.

95. Ibid., 210.

96. Ibid., 214.

97. Ibid., 135.

9. The Cottagers

98. Jackie Holland, "The African-American Presence on Martha's Vineyard," *Dukes County Intelligencer*, August 1991.
99. *Vineyard Style*, Summer 2021.
100. *Vineyard Gazette*, August 31, 1956.
101. *Vineyard Gazette*, September 6, 1957.
102. African-American Heritage Trail of Martha's Vineyard, "Cottagers' Corner," July 27, 2006, https://mvafricanamericanheritagetrail.org/trail-sites/cottagers-corner.
103. Ibid.
104. Louisa Hufstader, "Cottagers Join Harbor Homes in Homelessness Cause," *Vineyard Gazette*, February 14, 2022, https://vineyardgazette.com/news/2022/02/14/cottagers-join-harbor-homes-homelessness-cause.
105. *The Vine*, 2023, Island nonprofit directory.
106. *Vineyard Gazette*, August 18, 2023.
107. Hammond, *Dukes County Intelligencer*, 1991.
108. Lineage Asset Advisors, "What Is a Legacy Property?" February 14, 2018, https://lineageasset.com/what-is-a-legacy-property-series.
109. Noah Asimov, "Honoring the Legacy of Judge Herbert Tucker," *Vineyard Gazette*, July 22, 2018, https://vineyardgazette.com/news/2018/07/22/honoring-legacy-judge-herbert-tucker.
110. Linsey Lee, *Vineyard Voices Three: Words, Faces and Voices of Island People* (Edgartown, MA: Martha's Vineyard Museum, 2019), 278.
111. Lucas Thors, "Mary Tucker Dies Days before 103rd Birthday," *MV Times*, March 17, 2021, https://www.mvtimes.com/2021/03/17/mary-tucker-dies-days-103rd-birthday/.
112. "Service Saturday for Judge Herbert Tucker, Ambassador Abroad, Active on Vineyard," *Vineyard Gazette*, March 8, 2007, https://vineyardgazette.com/obituaries/2007/03/09/service-saturday-judge-herbert-tucker-ambassador-abroad-active-vineyard.
113. Thors, "Mary Tucker Dies."
114. Taylor, *Vineyard Gazette* town column, July 25, 2019.
115. *Vineyard Gazette*, August 25, 2003.
116. This family history was submitted by email from Barbara Edelin on August 27, 2023.
117. Ibid.

10. Fair Housing

118. *Boston Globe*, September 2023.
119. Taylor, *Race, Property, and the Power*, 245.
120. Edward W. Brooke, *Bridging the Divide: My Life* (New Brunswick, NJ: Rutgers University Press, 2006), 4.
121. Remax, "Edward Brooke's Legacy: Fair Housing for All," February 1, 2021, https://news.remax.com/edward-brookes-legacy-fair-housing-for-all.
122. Ibid.
123. Taylor, *Race, Property, and the Power*, 247.
124. Ibid., 262.
125. Lee, *Vineyard Voices Three*, 4.
126. Ibid., 2.

11. Black Business

127. Buildings of New England, "Aunt Georgia's House," August 5, 2020, https://buildingsofnewengland.com/tag/louisa-izett/.
128. Jacqueline Hammond, "The African-American Presence on Martha's Vineyard," *Dukes County Intelligencer*, August 1991.
129. Mia Vittimberga, "African American Heritage Trail Designates New Site," *MV Times*, July 27, 2023, https://www.mvtimes.com/2023/07/27/african-american-heritage-trail-designates-new-site/.
130. Discussion at the Oak Bluffs Library, August 3, 2023.

12. Black Culture

131. Brooke Kushwaha, "Vineyard History Is Food for Thought," *Vineyard Gazette*, June 5, 2023, https://vineyardgazette.com/news/2023/06/05/vineyard-history-food-thought.
132. Penelope Green, "An Island, A House, A Family, Summer," *New York Times*, July 3, 2005.
133. *Martha's Vineyard Magazine*, August 2023.

13. Black Politics

134. Taylor, *Race, Property and the Power*, 160.
135. Samantha J. Gross and Tal Kopan, "On Tony Martha's Vineyard a Center of Black Political Power Grows," *Boston Globe*, September 16, 2023, https://www.bostonglobe.com/2023/09/16/nation/tony-marthas-vineyard-center-black-political-power-grows/

14. Missteps

136. Brian MacQuarrie, "A Civil War Statue on Martha's Vineyard Has Sparked a Controversy," *Boston Globe*, May 3, 2019, https://www.bostonglobe.com/metro/2019/05/03/oak-bluffs-residents-want-plaque-honoring-confederate-soldiers-removed-civil-war-statue/INGnZn2DsD9Ey09SeH7neP/story.html.
137. Susannah Sudborough, "Oak Bluffs Select Board and NAACP Clash Over Flying Juneteenth Flag," Boston.com, June 14, 2022, https://www.boston.com/news/local-news/2022/06/14/oaks-bluffs-marthas-vineyard-juneteenth-flag-naacp/.
138. "Jack E. Robinson Dies at 79; Was Owner of Oak Bluffs Hotel," *Vineyard Gazette*, December 7, 2006, https://vineyardgazette.com/obituaries/2006/12/08/jack-e-robinson-dies-79-was-owner-oak-bluffs-hotel.
139. Emily Sweeney and Danny McDonald, "Police Investigating after Signs for a White Supremacist Group as Posted on Martha's Vineyard," September 5, 2023, https://www.bostonglobe.com/2023/09/05/metro/white-supremacist-group-signs-oak-bluffs/.
140. Lee, *Vineyard Voices Three*, 31.
141. Ibid.

15. Legacy Homeownership

142. Du Bois's double consciousness explored the duality Blacks experience in a racist society. It originated in his 1903 book of essays *The Souls of Black Folk*. Double consciousness reconciles African heritage with white society. It is how oppressed people react to controlling powers. Du Bois described it as "this sense of always looking at one's self through the eyes of others."
143. Email from Jennifer DaSilva on October 24, 2023.

BIBLIOGRAPHY

Brooke, Edward W. *Bridging the Divide: My Life*. New Brunswick, NJ: Rutgers University Press, 2006.

Coe, Jane Meleney. *A Guide to East Chop Families 2001*. Self-published, 2002.

Coe, Jane Meleney, and Rick Herrick. *2016 East Chop Families Guide*. Self-published, 2016.

Dresser, Thomas. *African Americans of Martha's Vineyard*. Charleston, SC: The History Press, 2010.

———. *The Rise of Tourism on Martha's Vineyard*. Charleston, SC: The History Press, 2020.

Dunbar, Erica. *Never Caught*. New York: Simon & Schuster, 2017.

Hare, Lloyd. *Martha's Vineyard: A Short History and Guide*. Edgartown, MA: Dukes County Historical Society, 1956.

Kahrl, Andrew. *The Land Was Ours*. Chapel Hill: University of North Carolina Press, 2016. eBook.

Lee, Linsey. *More Vineyard Voices: Words, Faces and Voices of Island People*. Edgartown, MA: Martha's Vineyard Historical Society, 2005.

———. *Vineyard Voices Three: Words, Faces and Voices of Island People*. Edgartown, MA: Martha's Vineyard Museum, 2019.

Mayhew, Eleanor Ransom. *Martha's Vineyard, A Short History and Guide*. Edgartown, MA: Dukes County Historical Society, 1956.

Melville, Gregory. *Over My Dead Body*. New York, NY: Harry N. Abrams, 2022.

Railton, Arthur. *The History of Martha's Vineyard*. Beverly, MA: Commonwealth Editions (in association with the Martha's Vineyard Historical Society), 2006.

Taylor, Richard. *Race, Property, and the Power of Place*. Cambridge, MA: Harvard Book Store, 2016.

Walton, Jocelyn Coleman. *The Place My Heart Calls Home: Stories of a Working Class African-American Family from Boston to Martha's Vineyard*. Weymouth, MA: A Nickel Down Publishing, 2018.

West, Dorothy. *The Living Is Easy*. Old Westbury, NY: Feminist Press, 1982. (originally published 1948).

———. *The Wedding*. New York: Doubleday Publishing, 1995.

Woo, Ilyon. *Master Slave Husband Wife: An Epic Journey from Slavery to Freedom*. New York: Simon & Schuster, 2023.

News and Periodicals

Boston Globe
Martha's Vineyard Magazine
Martha's Vineyard Museum Quarterly, formerly the *Dukes County Intelligencer*
Martha's Vineyard Times
The New Yorker
New York Times
Vineyard Gazette

INDEX

ABOUT THE AUTHORS

THOMAS DRESSER grew up in central Massachusetts and has made his home on Martha's Vineyard since the 1990s. After careers in teaching and nursing home administration, he drove school and tour buses, worked in nonprofits, and has written about Vineyard history.

He celebrated twenty-five years of marriage with high school classmate Joyce (Cournoyer) Dresser.

Thomas Dresser wrote *African Americans of Martha's Vineyard* in 2010. This is his sixteenth book with The History Press. Contact thomasdresser@gmail.com or thomasdresser.com for more information about his tours and books.

RICHARD L. TAYLOR has been a summer resident on Martha's Vineyard for over forty-five years and has become intimately involved in creating and advancing a range of Island programs and initiatives. He is the Oak Bluffs columnist for the *Vineyard Gazette* covering people, places, and events through the summer months. He is also the author of *Martha's Vineyard: Race, Property and the Power of Place*, published in 2016.

In his capacity as the President of the Union Chapel Educational and Cultural Institute he established the Charles Ogletree Public Forums. These programs feature engaging discussions among panelists addressing key issues of social justice, equity, philanthropy, and politics in July and August. He was a longtime Trustee at Union Chapel and he is now President Emeritus. His service to the Island was recognized when the Martha's Vineyard Museum bestowed on him the Martha's Vineyard Medal in 2023.

Visit us at
www.historypress.com